DO YOU

CARE

TO LEAD?

MICHAEL G. ROGERS

DO YOU

CARE

TO LEAD?

A 5-PART FORMULA FOR CREATING LOYAL AND RESULTS-FOCUSED TEAMS AND ORGANIZATIONS

WILEY

Published by John Wiley & Sons, Inc., Hoboken, New Jersey.
Published simultaneously in Canada.

For general information on our other products and services or for technical support, please contact our Customer Care Department within the United States at (800) 762-2974, outside the United States at (317) 572-3993 or fax (317) 572-4002.

Wiley publishes in a variety of print and electronic formats and by print-on-demand. Some material included with standard print versions of this book may not be included in e-books or in print-on-demand. If this book refers to media such as a CD or DVD that is not included in the version you purchased, you may download this material at http://booksupport.wiley.com. For more information about Wiley products, visit www.wiley.com.

Library of Congress Cataloging-in-Publication Data is Available:

ISBN 978-1-119-62841-5 (Hardcover)
ISBN 978-1-119-62846-0 (ePDF)
ISBN 978-1-119-62844-6 (ePub)

Cover Design: Wiley

Printed in the United States of America

10 9 8 7 6 5 4 3 2 1

This book is dedicated to all leaders—past, present, and future—who deeply care about those they lead. Thank you for your impact and positive influence on millions all over the world.

Contents

Introduction

In a *New York Times* interview, Charles Schwab CEO, Walt Bettinger, was asked what he learned in college. He chose to share one particular life changing experience that had a huge impact on him as both a businessman and leader.

Bettinger was a senior and preparing for the final exam in his business strategy class. At the time he had a 4.0 grade point average and had every intention of keeping that intact until graduation. He spent hours reviewing, studying, and memorizing formulas so that he could successfully do the calculations for the exam case studies.

As the teacher passed out the test, Bettinger noticed that it was on only one piece of paper. That surprised him because he thought surely it would be longer than that.

Once all students had received their exam, they were instructed to turn it over. Another surprise: both sides of the exam were blank. The professor said, "I've taught you everything I can teach you about business in the last 10 weeks, but the most important message, the most important question, is this: What's the name of the lady who cleans this building?"

Bettinger said, " … that had a powerful impact. It was the only test I ever failed, and I got the 'B' I deserved. Her name was Dottie, and I didn't know Dottie. I'd seen her, but I'd never taken the time to ask her name. I've tried to know every Dottie I've worked with ever since. It was a great reminder of what really matters in life, and that you should never lose sight of the people who do the real work."[1]

The title of this book—*Do You Care to Lead?*—is about two questions. First, *do you really care about leading*? Second, *do you really care about the people you lead*? They are two questions that every leader needs to ask, because if you don't want to lead, it will be next to impossible for you to really care about those you lead. And if you don't care about those you lead, then you probably shouldn't be leading.

This book is about becoming a Care to Lead Leader. It's about putting *caring* in the front seat of your leadership, where it belongs.

Care to Lead Leaders not only know Dottie's name but also her work-related hopes, aspirations, and challenges, and they humbly express appreciation for what she does for everyone, many of whom fail to appreciate her. Care to Lead Leaders are a unique breed of truly selfless, thoughtful, and caring leaders. Leadership is not about them; it was never about them. It is about the people whom they lead and work with, and whom they deeply care about.

During World War II, General Dwight D. Eisenhower, who later became the 34th president of the United States, was known to regularly walk among the troops. One day he noticed a younger soldier who was quiet and seemed down a bit.

He asked, "How are you feeling, son?"

"General," he said, "I'm awfully nervous. I was wounded two months ago, and just got back from the hospital yesterday. I don't feel so good."

Eisenhower said, "You and I are a great pair, then, because I'm nervous too … Maybe if we just walk along together to the river, we'll be good for each other."[2]

General Eisenhower was part of the Care to Lead Leader breed. He served this young soldier when the opportunity was presented. He opened up (vulnerability) in hopes that this young man would trust him. He was focused on nurturing and inspiring by walking with him. And he was committed to leading with his heart and those he led knew he cared. Each of these principles is at the core of the Care to Lead Leader Formula.

More people than ever are hungering for this type of leadership, but many leaders are missing the mark. In a Gallup survey, when employees were asked whether their supervisor or anyone else at work cared about them, only 4 out of 10 strongly agreed with that statement.[3] That lack of caring is startling. Although many leaders might say they care by speaking it with their lips, unfortunately they are far from caring with their heart.

When practiced, Care to Lead Leadership makes a significant difference in people's work life and the companies they work for. Studies show that employees who felt they were part of a loving and caring culture at work reported higher levels of satisfaction and teamwork compared to those that didn't.[4] And statements such as "Management shows a sincere interest in me as a person, not just an employee" is an important differentiator between companies making the top 10 in Fortune's top 100 annual Best Companies to Work For list and the other 90 that didn't.[5] Caring about people matters.

If employees desire to be cared more about and leaders and organizations can benefit from caring more, but only 4 in 10 feel they are actually cared about, what are leaders missing? They are missing the right focus in most cases. In a survey conducted by Economist.com; C-suite executives most frequently stated that technology and finance were the two areas that they most wanted to improve. However, when lower-ranking employees were asked what skills they wished their top executives would get better at, they most often answered leadership and emotional intelligence.[6] Executives were not anywhere near the same page in how they responded. What leaders think they need isn't what those they lead want and need from them. Although technology and finance are important, they aren't as important as the people you lead. Business is about the people who do the business. If you fail to care about those you lead, those you lead will eventually fail to care about results and also eventually fail to be loyal to you, your team, and the organization.

Unfortunately, too many "leaders" are stuck in the old styles of leadership: a top-down approach with little care and value placed on the people "below." Such leaders are concerned only about themselves. I have had such leaders in my life and have consulted with some. Perhaps you have had a leader or two like this in your career. They lead by fear more than with their heart. Many tend to anger easy, throw their fists down, make demands, talk tough, are generally negative, and seem to always be upset about something. Their only open-door policy is to shut the door if someone sees it open. Those they manage as a result go out of their way trying to avoid them and do just enough to stay out of trouble. And when they have an opportunity, most of these people being managed by such leaders leave the second they have a chance.

I have also had my share of "leaders" and consulted with many more who, although not necessarily focused on creating fear, were more focused on numbers and processes rather than people. These types of leaders tended to listen less. They lacked a vision for their team(s), there was little connection, and there was unfortunately a lot of apathy. Those being led by these types of leaders simply checked out.

* * *

Care to Lead Leaders take people on rocket rides. Managers, such as those previously described, take their people on subway rides. Subways are boring, predictable, and uninspiring. You will be hard-pressed to find people who smile on subway rides. It's the same thing, to the same place, every day. It takes very little coaxing to get people to board them because, similar to robots, they simply do what they are told or what they always do, day in and day out. It's easy to get people from destination A to B, but they never really get from C through Z. People just don't care much about the destination; they are more focused on just getting things done, doing barely enough to collect a paycheck and then going home.

Care to Lead Leaders know that rocket rides are a lot more exciting and inspiring, and the results are so much more impactful to teams, organizations, and the lives of the people they lead. Rockets get people to places they have never been before and those who take the ride get to do things they have never done before. People in rockets stay inspired, achieve much more, and never want to get off the ride—they are loyal through and through. Care to Lead Leaders understand that the best way to get people on rockets is to show the way and then get out of the way. They lead from the bottom-up, not top-down. They aren't micromanagers; they deeply care enough to do exactly what they need to do to inspire people to become everything they are capable of becoming and everything and more that their teams and organizations need them to become.

Most people want to be a part of something bigger, challenging, and exciting. They want to go to places they never believed they could or would. And every leader has an important responsibility to those they lead and the organizations and companies they belong to to get them there.

This book is about giving you the right formula for getting those you lead to take rocket rides. The time has arrived for you to become a Care to Lead Leader—that's how people board rockets. That's how leaders generate fiercely loyal and results-focused teams. Becoming a Care to Lead Leader is going to forever change you, your teams, and organizations, but you must be willing to learn and carefully follow and apply the five-part SONIC formula of **S**erve, **O**pen (up), **N**urture, **I**nspire, and **C**ommit. The following chapters are focused on showing you how.

Notes

1. Adam Bryant, "You've Got to Open Up to Move Up," *New York Times,* February 6, 2016, BU 2.
2. John Wukovits, *Eisenhower: A Biography (Great Generals)* (New York: Palgrave Macmillan Trade, 2006), 157.
3. Gallup, *State of the American Workplace* (Washington, DC: Gallup Inc., 2017), 108.
4. Sigal G. Barsade and Olivia A. O'Neill, "What's Love Got to Do with It? A Longitudinal Study of the Culture of Companionate Love and Employee and Client Outcomes in a Long-Term Care Setting," *Administrative Science Quarterly* 59, no. 4 (December 2014): 551–98, doi:10.1177/0001839214538636.
5. Jason Slusher, "Corporate Culture: Love Is All You Need," *Great Place to Work,* February 14, 2017, https://www .greatplacetowork.com/resources/blog/corporate-culture-love-is-all-you-need.
6. Natalie Baker, "Your Employees Wish You Were Emotionally Intelligent," *The Economist,* n.d., https:// execed.economist.com/blog/industry-trends/your-employees-wish-you-were-emotionally-intelligent.

Chapter 1

Serve

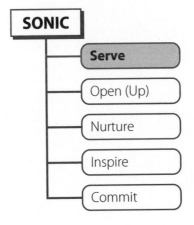

If serving is below you, leadership is beyond you.

—Anonymous

The first part of the Caring to Lead Leader Formula is to serve. You won't get those you lead to even think about following you unless you serve. Pouring a big portion of this selfless action into your leadership is the magic sauce of Care to Lead Leaders. It's the first ingredient of connection between you and your team and organization. And it is the fastest way, hands down, leaders can connect and start building trust with their people. Service starts with your personal commitment to selflessness.

Selflessness

An anthropologist was studying the culture of a remote African tribe. On the final days of his studies he had prepared to leave and was waiting for transportation to take him to the airport. While waiting, the children of this tribe had gathered around him as they had done many times before.

The anthropologist decided to gather the candy he had collected from a town he had visited on his way to the remote tribe days before. He filled a basket with the sweets and then placed it underneath a fairly large tree. He then walked about

100 or so yards from the tree and drew a line in the dirt. The children were told that when he said go, they were to run as fast as they could and that the first one to the basket would win all of the candy for themselves.

The anthropologist gave the signal and then something surprisingly happened. The children held hands and ran to the tree together. Once there, they excitedly sat in a circle and shared the candy. The anthropologist was a bit shocked. He asked them why they all went together when one of them could have had all of the candy for him- or herself.

A younger girl in the group looked up at him and said, "How can one of us be happy if all the others are sad?"

Africans use a term called *Ubuntu*. It means "I am, because we are." Desmond Tutu, the well-known South African human rights activist, said of *Ubuntu*, "It speaks of the very essence of being human. When we want to give high praise to someone we say, *Yu, u nobuntu;* hey, so-and-so has *Ubuntu*. Then you are generous, you are hospitable, and you are friendly and caring and compassionate. You share what you have. It is to say, my humanity is caught up, inextricably bound up, in yours. We belong in a bundle of life."[1] *Ubuntu* is at the very core of Care to Lead Leaders and what they do as they work on building team and organizational cultures focused on selflessness and service.

Ubuntu is everything that a leader should commit to and aspire to practice, to be, and to create. Like the little girl who so sweetly answered the anthropologist, it's about your personal selflessness: caring about and putting others first. It is realizing that you are not a leader without those you lead.

You are a leader because others have chosen to follow you, not because you were simply appointed to be such. Because of that you have an important and even sacred responsibility to selflessly **serve** those you lead with all of your heart, might, mind, soul, and strength. You aren't superior to others; you are dependent on them as much as they are dependent on you. Leadership is not about you; it is about each of you. That's the essence of *Ubuntu* and it is the way of life for Care to Lead Leaders.

As you commit to and practice selflessness as a Care to Lead Leader, your leadership naturally instills and creates *Ubuntu* types of cultures on your teams and in your organizations. Service becomes a priority, and team and organizational concerns about each other's needs is foundational to who you become together. Everyone is more focused on what they can do together than what they can do alone. Egos, money, and career aspirations take a back seat to the success of the entire team. There is no such thing as a solitary individual. When one succeeds, it is the success of everyone, because everyone had a role in it. Can you imagine the power of teams, organizations, and even entire nations practicing *Ubuntu,* with such a large focus on selflessly serving one another? It is a complete and powerful game changer for sure.

Creating such cultures of selflessness and service starts with you, and it always starts with you, as I will highlight now and several times throughout this chapter. Personally focusing on selfless service is the key to unlocking Care to Lead Leadership.

Service Unlocks Leadership

Not too long ago, I was speaking at Southwest Airlines. The airline, as you might know, has a strong culture and reputation of caring and service that many other companies have tried to replicate over the years. Although historically the airline industry has lost money, Southwest Airlines has amazingly turned a profit year after year. As I spoke to many of the employees there, I quickly learned that much of that success has had to do with their deep connection to their history, culture, and a focus on serving each other, which started with their cofounder and past CEO, Herb Kelleher. He was a model of what he hoped the culture at Southwest would create.

Author Ekaterina Walter shares an interesting story on Inc .com of a friend, Gregg Gregory, who was once on the same Southwest flight that Kelleher was on. With a giant Mickey Mouse baseball hat on, Gregory had noticed the CEO way up front in the boarding line. Although he thought it kind of cool, he didn't really think much more about it, until Kelleher walked by him on the plane taking a seat all the way at the back and then plopping himself in a middle seat. As you may or may not know, the back of the plane and a middle seat for most passengers are the least coveted spots and seats on the entire plane.

As the aircraft reached a safe altitude, Gregory watched Kelleher walk to the front of the plane where he began chatting with airline attendants for a little while. The CEO then made his way down the aisle and started assisting flight attendants by serving peanuts and beverages to passengers.

Walter writes, "Eventually he came up to Gregory's seat and said, 'Hi. My name is Herb Kelleher. Thank you for flying my airline. Can I get you something to drink?'"[2]

Herb Kelleher's actions on that flight was what Care to Lead Leaders do. Service is a way of life for Care to Lead Leaders, and as mentioned previously, it spreads throughout their teams and organizations. It's something they do without thinking about because it is something they always do. They are regularly asking themselves, what can I do to help someone, what can I do to cheer someone else up, what can I do to make something easier for others, what can I do to inspire those I lead? They deeply understand that they need and depend on those they lead as much as their people need them, and those they lead know this. *Ubuntu*!

Selfless service signals a number of things in your leadership to others. It conveys that you care, that you can be trusted, that you are approachable, that you have wisdom and direction others can benefit from, and that you are someone to be followed. In other words, **your service to your teams and organizations is your key to unlocking your leadership**. In fact, as mentioned previously, it's the quickest way there is to establishing trust in others and yourself as a leader.

Service is fundamental to the rest of the Care to Lead Leader Formula. As with all formulas, you can't miss this part; it is the key ingredient to everything else. It is a staple. The other parts of the formula in this book are deeply connected to the principle of selfless service, as I highlight in the following chapters.

Service Changes Hearts, and Changed Hearts Change People, Teams, and Organizations

I have always found it amazing how service changes people and as a result people change the world around them. It's why we have a Global Youth Service Day, International Volunteer Day, National Volunteer Week, and Random Acts of Kindness Week, to name a few. It's also the reason we have wonderful organizations dedicated to service, such as the Lion's Clubs International, Kiwanis, and the Rotary Club. It's because we as a world understand that service changes hearts, and changed hearts together change all of us. It can even change the heart of an enemy.

The Civil War was one of the most ugly and vicious wars in American history. At least 620,000 men lost their lives in battle, which was approximately 2.5% of the entire population of the country at the time. Total casualties exceeded those of all other American wars, from the Revolution through Vietnam.

In winter 1862 one of the most decisive and bloodiest battles of the Civil War was fought in Fredericksburg, Virginia. One in 10 Union soldiers had lost his life, though the Union soldiers far outnumbered their confederate adversary. When US president Abraham Lincoln got word of the casualties, he was quoted as crying, "If there is a worse place than hell, I am in it."

The campaign in Fredericksburg had initially looked promising for the Union Army, but it quickly turned bad after many blunderings and red tape delays. On December 13, 1862, Union forces attacked the Confederates at Marye's Heights, a large sloping hill overlooking the town of Fredericksburg. The Confederate army had fortified themselves against a stone wall that ran along the crest of the hill, sitting four deep and out of the sight of the Union army.

As the Union army began their advance, they were viciously ambushed by the hiding Confederates. By the morning of December 14, more than 12,000 Union soldiers were injured or fell at the hands of the Confederate army; not a single Union soldier made it to the wall and very few Union soldiers came within 50 yards of their firing adversaries.

Many of those remaining on the battlefield were still alive, but they suffered from wounds, cold, and thirst. During that long night, both sides were forced to listen to the cries and moans of those soldiers still living. Several described these cries to be "weird, unearthly, terrible to hear and bear." Listening to these men who were "lying crippled on a hillside so many miles from home—broke the hearts of soldiers on both sides of the battlefield."[3]

Richard Rowland Kirkland, a 19-year old infantry sergeant for the Confederacy, could not bear to listen to the suffering soldiers any longer. That morning, he asked his commanding officer if he could scale the wall and provide water for the suffering Union troops who could be seen strewn across the battlefield. The young sergeant exclaimed to his commanding officer, "All night and all day I have heard those poor people crying for water. Water! Water! And I can't stand it any longer. I come to ask permission to go and give them water."[4]

The commanding officer initially denied Kirkland's request because of the danger, but with Kirkland's persistence he later granted him permission. With several canteens hung around his neck and to the astonishment of men on both sides, Kirkland climbed the wall to provide much needed help. Several shots were instantly fired, thinking that Kirkland's motives were to wound more. However, after realizing what was happening, the shooting quickly ceased.

Sergeant Kirkland made his way to each soldier, comforting them the best he could by laying his jacket over one and providing water to the thirsty lips of another. For the next hour and a half, he would scale the wall a number of times with his canteens to get more water for his enemy as cries of "Water, please water, for God's sake water" could be heard all over the field. It was a heartfelt and loving act of service that stopped a vicious war for just a moment.

The Union Army was actually planning to make another attack that morning; however, they decided otherwise and marched a different direction. Many attribute the Union Army's changed heart to the selfless hero who risked his life to aid an enemy whom he had risked his life to defeat the day before. Sergeant Richard Kirkland's actions changed the hearts of men on both sides. Regardless of what position you took or side you were on, I believe every soldier was different from that day forward because of the selfless service of Sergeant Richard Kirkland. He became known on both sides as the Angel of Marye's Heights.

Service changes hearts, and changed hearts change teams and organizations and even entire armies. You may not ever be asked to risk your life for someone you lead, let alone an enemy. However, service is a tool that you can regularly use to turn your heart toward those you lead and to turn their hearts toward you and toward each other, even the hearts of your adversary.

I told my children as they were growing up that the fastest way to make a friend out of someone you don't like, or to make a friend out of someone who doesn't like you, is to serve. One kind act, even one simple kind act, can change the way others feel about you. Service has the ability to strongly influence every relationship that you have as a leader, both on your team(s) and in your organization(s).

On occasion I teach part-time in the school of business at the university in the town I live. I give an assignment to students each semester in which I ask them to share with me how service has changed a team they belonged to. One student shared with me a project team that she had been assigned to in school. She said that this team consisted of a mix of strong and diverse personalities and that there was personal conflict almost from day one. Teammates started showing up late for meetings and turning in their portions of the work late, which of course had downstream effects for the rest of the team. She was worried that this was going to end badly and that they were going to get a failing grade.

One evening during class it had been snowing rather hard. As she was walking out to her car, she didn't look forward to scraping and brushing the snow off of her windows. But as she got closer, she noticed to her relief that her windows had already been cleared of snow. She stopped and looked around the parking lot to see who had done such a kind thing and spotted one of her teammates going around scraping and brushing the snow off of the cars of each of her project teammates! From that day forward the hearts of everyone on that team changed she said. Teammates started caring more about each other and as a result caring more about the project. The team ended up with a much better grade than she had thought they would. **One teammate's choice to lead through service changed the hearts and performance of this project team.**

Several years ago, I was speaking with a client who was the leader and business owner of a growing company. He had shared how at one time he did not like his job very much. He even started dreading coming into the office each morning. "I liked everything about what I did, except for the people problems," he said. *I can see some of you right now nodding your heads and saying yep!* Tired of the gossip, negative attitudes, and having employees regularly coming to him complaining about what others had done or said, he was at his wits' end. That all changed, when one member of his team made the choice to start serving others. When this teammate had finished her work and sometimes just at the end of the day, she would ask others what she could do to help them. Her service became contagious and over time others on the team started asking what they could do to help each other. To his surprise hearts began to change and the team as a whole began to change as well. Negative interactions began to be replaced slowly with more positive interactions and he started getting his sanity back! **One person's choice to lead through service changed the hearts of a team and changed this owner's company.**

When Rodney King was assaulted by four policemen and each of the four officers were then acquitted, community anger turned into horrible violence and significant property damage. The 1992 Los Angeles riots resulted in 63 deaths,

2,383 injuries, approximately 12,000 arrests, and close to 3,600 buildings set on fire with 1,100 being totally destroyed. There were times that calls were coming in every minute of another building being set on fire.

I was a student in college at the time living in Southern California. I clearly remember the live footage of fires, devastation, protests, arrests, and of many angry people throughout the Los Angeles metropolitan area. It was a scary moment when civility and quiet protests quickly gave way to complete disorder, mobs, looting, brutality, and bloodshed.

However, in the heart of the riots in South Central Los Angeles and surrounded by destruction and smoldering buildings, five McDonald's restaurants were left completely unscathed. Not a window broken or a single streak of spray paint could be found on any part of these five buildings. A miracle? No, not really. The entrepreneurs and leaders of these McDonald's restaurants were servants in the community. They had given hundreds of basketballs away to youth groups and basketball centers in this economically poor area. They had given hundreds of free cups of coffee every morning to homeless men. They also created jobs and put in place literacy programs. When people were asked why they had left the McDonald's buildings untouched during the riots, they responded by saying that those businesses were like one of them and were always looking after the community. **A group of leaders and entrepreneurs who made the choice to lead through service had softened the hearts of a community toward their businesses, which in turn saved five of their restaurants from destruction.**

Serve

What impact will you have when you choose to regularly serve? What hearts do you have the opportunity to soften and change? How can you as a Care to Lead Leader not only serve more to connect at a deeper level but also to get your team to serve more and connect at unprecedented levels? The answers to these questions start with your understanding of why service works.

The Magic of Service (The Service Effect)

What is going on that makes service magically work on teams and in organizations? I have noticed for years that if I was a bit moody or even feeling a little down, that if I forgot myself and did something kind for someone else, my mood would change instantly. I didn't quite understand why, but it was a great tool for getting me out of any funk I was in. Perhaps you have noticed the same thing. This is the very reason therapists have used service through volunteering as a way to combat depression.

I also discovered that service changed how I felt toward others and oftentimes how they felt about me. There is a strong correlation between service and caring. The more we serve, the more we care, and the more we care, the greater desire we have to serve. I particularly have noticed this in a variety of leadership positions I have held. The more I consciously served those I was leading, the happier I was, the greater caring connection I made, and the stronger our team and organizations became.

I started calling this the *service effect*. It is the reason for the change you begin to see on teams and in organizations and companies that make service a priority. It's the very reason why, as talked about previously, service changes hearts, and changed hearts change teams. It connects people and entire groups of people in ways that nothing else can. It benefits teams, customers, and even families. Entire cultures within organizations are built on creating this service effect, and the positives of such focus are difficult to deny.

A study was conducted by the Great Place to Work organization of several hundred companies and more than 380,000 employees. The research showed that companies who made giving back through service a priority were associated with greater employee retention, higher levels of brand ambassadorship on the part of workers, and more enthusiastic employees. Staffers who believe their organizations give back to the community are a striking 13 times more likely to look forward to coming to work compared to employees who do not perceive their employers to be generous toward the community.[5]

We just feel better about companies, organizations, teams, and leaders that are focused on serving. The reason is due to the service effect and its three connecting components; *connection*, *reciprocity*, and *multiplicity* (figure 1.1). There is scientific research to back up each one.

Connection

The first phase of the *service effect* begins with the act of service. You are probably familiar with Charles Dickens's classic story, "A Christmas Carol." An elderly curmudgeon by the name of Ebenezer Scrooge is the focal point of the story. He is mean, lacks any type of giving spirit, and is obsessed with

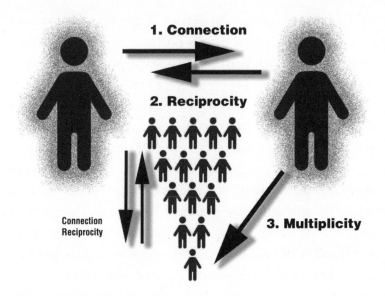

Figure 1.1 The Service Effect

his own personal gain. Scrooge is a miserable person, as any person who focuses entirely on himself would be. However, on the night of Christmas Eve he is given a second chance to redeem his sad mortal life in the form of three Christmas spirits. The ghosts of Christmas past, Christmas present, and Christmas yet to come take him on a personal eye-opening journey. When Scrooge wakes up Christmas morning, he is a changed man. As a result, he makes amends to those he had wronged before by doing a number of selfless good deeds for others. Service is now his focus, and he becomes the opposite of what he was in his past. He becomes filled with love and a lot of giddiness and laughter.

When we make the choice to serve others with pure motives and not expect anything in return it feels not only

Do You Care to Lead?

right but good, too. Ebenezer Scrooge was experiencing what is called the *helper's high* or the *giver's glow*. His kind deeds felt unlike anything he had experienced before. Science shows that when we selflessly give to others we are flooded by powerful neurochemicals, such as endorphins (released to help our nervous system cope with pain and stress), dopamine (helps us take action toward our goals), serotonin (helps us feel significant and important), and oxytocin (creates trust, cooperation, and connection). This quartet of chemicals is the factor behind happiness. No wonder we feel so good when we are helping others! These chemicals are not only released by the act of service but also when vicariously watching someone serve, anticipating service, or recalling something kind we did for someone.

What does this mean for you as a leader and those you lead? Serving others has the potential to connect you to the people you lead in deeper and more meaningful ways due to these neurochemicals, specifically, oxytocin—the same connection chemical released when a mother feeds her baby. As a leader you want to personally create connections with those you lead. Connection leads to greater trust, empathy, and loyalty between you and those you lead. It also creates greater trust, empathy, and loyalty between and across your teams and within organizations. Connection is the foundation and fabric to effective leadership.

Serving your team puts into motion real changes to the team(s) and organization(s) you lead. As you start to feel a deeper connection with those you serve, they begin to feel a deeper connection with you. This is in large part due to reciprocity.

Reciprocity

In 1974, Phillip Kunz and his family received more Christmas cards than they had ever received in the past. They came regularly each day and sometimes they were receiving up to a dozen cards a day. The cards came in all types of shapes, sizes, and assortments, and some included handwritten notes and pictures of recent graduations and new homes. The basic message was the same: those sending the cards wanted the Kuntz family to know that they were cared about.

This all seems normal, except that Phillip and his family did not know any of those who sent a card. They were complete strangers!

Kunz was a sociologist at Brigham Young University. Earlier that year he had decided to send out some 600 Christmas cards to see what would happen. He got around 200 back! People felt obligated to give back to Phillip because he had given to them.

Years ago, disciples of the Hare Krishna religious group would give flowers at airports to raise money for their movement. They stood outside of gates in the airport terminals, and when people were coming off the plane, they would give tired passengers a little orange flower and say that it was a gift. When the weary passenger took the flower, they would be kindly asked for a donation. With the flower in hand, it was difficult not to give back.

In 1976, the *New York Times* had interviewed a security guard at Chicago's O'Hare airport who was charged with regulating solicitors. He said that on average each Krishna was making $120 to $150 a day.[6] The Hare Krishna movement was killing it financially in the seventies by making people feel obligated to give back due to an act of service.

What Phillip Kunz and the Hare Krishna group had discovered was the power of what social psychology refers to as the law of reciprocity. It is considered by some to be the most powerful law of humankind. If you can learn to create reciprocity through service in your leadership and on your teams and organizations, you have the opportunity to create powerful cultures of connection where your people are focused on others, including your team, first.

Of course, in most cases, we shouldn't expect something in return when we serve. Doing so negates all of the wonderful benefits in the connection component we just talked about. But, when we serve, there is a good chance that others will want to give back to us.

The law of reciprocity also responds to not only what you do but also what you say:

"I love what you have done with this project; we couldn't have done it without you."

"Thank you for taking the time to help me with the budget; you are so good at making things easier."

"I always enjoy working with you because of how positive you are."

Whenever you give a genuine and specific compliment and make others feel good about themselves (acts of service in their own right), those you compliment deposit what you said somewhere in their mind and feel a need to reciprocate your thoughtfulness back at some point. This is how relationships and connections are created.

There is this constant need that we have to be "even" with others. In their book, *The Imperial Animal*,[7] authors Lionel Tiger and Robin Fox claim that as humans we live in a "web of indebtedness." This web of indebtedness is at the heart of the service effect. It's what sets into motion the magic of service.

When Care to Lead Leaders step up and do kind things, others want to step up and serve as well. They want to give back. As they give back, the same neurochemicals that were released when you served are released in them when they serve. They feel the same things you are feeling and the connection between you and those you serve considerably deepens as you strive to give back to each other. Service generates more service and your people become more loyal to you, the team, and organization as a result. But it doesn't end with just those you serve. The effects are multiplied.

Multiplicity

Multiplicity is the effect service has on a team or organization when service begins to influence and inspire those beyond the people initially affected directly by the service. When you do a kind act for others, they not only want to do something nice in return but they also want to do nice things for others. The effect is a multiplicity of good feelings and service. A culture of "paying it forward" begins to take shape and it ripples throughout your organization.

Economists have conducted a number of studies to show in principle why this works. They use a game called the *Public*

Goods Game. Breaking into groups, participants are given a certain amount of money and the choice to either keep their money or put it secretly into a public pot. People are aware that the money put into the public pot will eventually be doubled and divided among all group members regardless of whether someone put money in the pot or not. If a participant chooses to keep the money, she benefits from keeping not only what she held on to but also receives a share of what she gets from the divided doubled public pot—getting in essence a bonus due to the generosity of others. The game goes on for multiple rounds.

In one particular experiment, groups of four volunteers were put together to play the game for a total of six rounds. After each round, players were told what their groupmates had contributed, but identities were kept secret. Additionally, groups were shuffled each round to ensure players didn't play with each other more than once. What researchers found is interesting and explains the effect of service multiplicity on teams and in organizations.

In this experiment, each act of generosity, when players chose to put money into the public pot, influenced three other players in the group to give more money in the next round. And here is where the power of multiplicity takes hold—each of these three players also influenced the people they played with later creating a ripple effect of more acts of generosity.

Service to Results

The key for Care to Lead Leaders is to take action now and start selflessly serving. Your kind and generous acts of service are the start to changing your culture and creating a multiplicity of goodness. When you begin to regularly think of others, the magic begins to happen. That was the case for entrepreneur, angel investor, public speaker, mentor, and philanthropist Amy Rees Anderson. In a *Forbes* article written by Anderson,[8] she shares a story that demonstrates the power of what one leader can create and how that is multiplied not only across an organization but across a customer base as well.

During her time as CEO of a past company that Anderson had founded, she began to notice that holidays were great for some of her employees and not so great for others who were going through hard times. She creatively thought of ways she could help everyone to have a happy holiday. Anderson said, "I realized that as the leader I had the ability to get the employees focused on helping each other over the holidays by launching what [was] called our company 'Santa Store.'"

The Santa Store became a game changer in her organization. The way it worked was that during the holiday season, employees who were able were asked to go through their things at home and determine if there was anything that they didn't need any longer and contribute them to the store. Employees were then told that they could take any items from the store that they needed. It was a chance to both give and receive. Anderson said, "We had employees donating everything from kids' clothing to adult clothing, to toys, DVDs, video games, winter coats, gloves, computers, bicycles, televisions, DVD players, furniture, books, games … you name it, we had it donated."

There was no limit to what employees could take from the tables of the store; however, they were asked to only take the things they truly needed for their families so that there was an assurance that employees' families were taken care of first. Once employees had enough to make sure their families were taken care of, they made time for them to look through what was left and take what they thought might help someone else in need that year. This became a great thing for everyone, but as Anderson explains, it didn't stop there.

She said through employees giving compassionately to others in need, the morale of the company started to improve. "People were happier at work, they were kinder to one another, and then suddenly that ripple effect began spreading beyond the walls of our company." For example, employees on phones started showing much higher levels of care and concern for their customer's needs, which resulted in more focus on how they could make their customers happy. Employees started going the extra mile and sending personal handwritten thank-you notes to customers, and as a result Anderson said, "over time we saw these clients begin to go the extra mile for us as well. They began referring more business to us, both from their own organizations as well as from other organizations. As a result, our company began to grow and flourish in ways we couldn't have imagined and the impact to our bottom line was amazing."

One leader, one creative service idea, and the determination of that leader to make it happen across her organization affected not only people but results as well through the service effect of connection, reciprocity, and multiplicity. Service is magical when it starts with you—your teams and organizations as a result become service-focused, not self-focused. When this happens, you create a culture of service that includes strong feelings of connection and community. What's your idea to make this happen on your team(s) and organization(s)?

The Practice of Service

The effects of service on you, your teams, and organizations sound great, right? But ... what do you do? Where do you start? How do you find ways to serve? How do you make service a habit? You start by having the right heart, becoming aware of opportunities, regularly reminding yourself of opportunities, and making time for opportunities.

Having the Right Heart

Doing service for the right reasons is as important as the act of service itself. Service can be as selfish as it is selfless. If serving isn't done for the right reasons, it will have the wrong conclusions. It has to come from the heart. It has to come from a place of genuinely caring about others and putting them first. The motive for serving others as a leader can't be done for example to "one-up" someone, or with the hope that others will see and perceive you as an angel. People see right through impure motives, and you can do more damage than good. When done the right way, all of the magic behind service is quickly realized.

You might be thinking at this point, "I don't have the energy to serve more" or "I don't have the time to serve more" or "how do I even get the desire to serve more?" If you don't have energy, do it any way. If you don't have time, do it any way. If you want more desire, then just do it. Are you seeing a theme? Just do it! Because service to your team propels them to new heights in trust and connection, you have to do it. Your leadership requires you to do it. Service must become a priority.

At first it might not seem very genuine, maybe a bit forced, but that quickly changes the more you serve. There is wisdom as it relates to service in simply faking it until you make it, or even better, faking it until you become it. Yes, initially you may do it because it's the right thing to do not because you want to do it. You might do it a little begrudgingly. But over time experiencing the effects (connection, reciprocity, and multiplicity) of service is altruistically addicting because of how it makes you feel and seeing how it affects and changes those you lead, your team, and organization.

Pause, Reflect, and Apply

- When you serve, how often are you doing it because you genuinely care and want to do it as opposed to doing it because you have to or for some other reason?

  _____

  _____

  _____

- What do you need to change in terms of how you approach service and how will you change it?

  _____

  _____

  _____

Becoming Aware of Opportunities

Opportunities to serve are plentiful; we just need to look, ask, and listen.

Look Being aware of opportunities is usually the result of looking for opportunities. Opportunities to serve are all around us. When 13-year-old Natalie Gilbert lost her words while singing the US national anthem in front of 20,000 NBA fans in Portland, Oregon, Trailblazers coach Maurice Cheeks stepped in and helped.

Gilbert had managed to get through about 20 seconds of the song before she began to stumble.

"O say can you see, by the dawn's early light," she started. "What so proudly we hailed, at the starlight's ... star ... "

With a nervous and awkward smile in what had to be by far the most embarrassing moment of her young life, Gilbert tossed her head from one side to the other trying to shake it off. The arena became silent as she looked around trying to figure out what to do, desperately looking for anyone to help. Within seconds Cheeks decided to step in and come to her aid.

"It's alright, come on, come on," he said as he put his arm around her and raised the mic to her mouth.

He then picked up where she had left off and suddenly, she had the courage to finish the rest of the anthem. With the coach's encouragement, the crowd and each of the players from both teams also joined in and Gilbert seemed to receive more and more strength as she finished.

The thoughtful and compassionate service of this leader not only had an impact on young Natalie Gilbert but also the crowd and players in attendance and the millions of others watching it live. Did those who witness this feel a little more kindness in their hearts that evening? Do you think that others felt inspired enough to do a good turn for someone else that night? Absolutely! After the game that evening assistant Dallas Maverick's coach, Del Harris, walked into Cheeks's office with tears in his eyes—touched and inspired by what he had witnessed. He was later quoted as saying, "Anybody that has any feelings at all had to have an emotional reaction."[9]

The great news is that Gilbert went on to perform many times after that and to even study music. I am sure a big part of that could be attributed to a leader who cared enough to step in when an opportunity presented itself. That's what Care to Lead Leaders do. When they find an opportunity, they don't watch from the sidelines; they jump in.

Ask Finding opportunities is sometimes as simple as asking. I personally have always loved the simple question "What can I do to ease your burden?" I call it a *superpower question.* A burden could be anything from not understanding how to do something to a crisis at home. But it's a question that will begin to uncover things you might have never found if you hadn't asked. Once you know, you can serve. I have been fortunate to have leaders in my life who have asked me this question. Even if there wasn't anything I immediately needed at the moment, my shoulders seemed to be lighter knowing that I had someone who cared enough to ask and was there if I needed them.

Imagine the trust and connection you would create with those you lead if you were to regularly ask, "What can I do to ease your burden?" What if you started by asking this question to the person who cleans your building? It would probably shock that person, but he or she would start to immediately feel more valued and supported, right? Absolutely! And imagine what it would do if others happened to see you, a leader in the organization, showing more concern and helping with even the humblest of job responsibilities. Think about it: not only do you know the cleaner's name but also you took the time to serve and make that person feel important. That is a service ripple just waiting to happen.

Listen Those you lead are going to regularly drop hints of ways you can help. Care to Lead Leaders carefully listen and find opportunities to make an immediate difference in someone's life. The problem with most of us is that we are so busy with "big" and "important" things that we forget to take the time to be busy carefully listening to the things that matter most long term in our leadership. And listening means just that. Giving lip service by asking, but failing to really listen, lessens the chance that those being asked will give a meaningful response. More on listening in chapter 3.

Pause, Reflect, and Apply

- Are you looking, asking, and listening? On a scale of 1 to 10, with 10 being the highest, how good are you at all three?

  _____

  _____

  _____

- What is one specific thing you will start doing in the next five days to find more opportunities to serve?

  _____

  _____

  _____

Regularly Reminding Yourself of Opportunities

Regularly thinking about others means that you have to create a habit of always thinking about others. Here are three fairly simple and practical ways that you can make service more of a habit.

Keep a Service Journal Introspection is a key way to improving and creating lasting habits. Some leaders have found that keeping a service journal helps them. The idea behind a service journal is simply introspecting daily on your service to others. Each evening you ask what you did, the impact it made or is going to make on others, the impact it made on you, and what types of future service opportunities you have identified. By asking and answering these questions you begin to create a mind-set focused on putting others first. Service starts to become a priority and eventually a habit. It's a simple thing to do, but it has powerful and lasting results and is a critical practice of Care to Lead Leaders.

You can get a free template of my Care to Lead Leader service journal at www.doyoucaretolead.com/tools.

Transfer Marbles I once read about a CEO of a fairly large company who struggled with complimenting others. He decided to get a handful of different marbles and put them in his pocket. Each day when he had specifically, genuinely paid someone a compliment, he would transfer one of the marbles to the other pocket. His goal at the end of each night was to have filled his pocket with the marbles that signified a compliment and then start all over the next day. Complimenting others (an act of service, which we will talk more about in chapter 4) eventually became a habit and had a positive effect in many lives. Keeping the needs of others at the top of your mind can be as easy as transferring marbles every time you do something of service for someone else.

Place Quotes and Pictures Another way to create a service habit is by putting physical reminders of service around your workspace. Here are some suggestions:

- There are many quotes of service that you could use to inspire you to serve every day. Find a quote, print it in large font in a document, and place it where you will regularly see it.

- Place a picture of the team(s) and organization(s) you serve. If you focus on doing something kind for someone in the picture every day, eventually every time you look at it, it will act as a reminder.

- Place a copy of *Do You Care to Lead?* where you will see it every day. I especially like this one 😊. This is also easy to do, because you already have the book.

- Place a picture of a selfless servant you admire on your desk. The picture could be someone in the past, a historical figure, or even a boss who was an example of a service leader to you.

- Create something or purchase something with the word *service* and place it in a prominent place.

Physical reminders help us create positive habits. Over time, regularly thinking about others first becomes a regular part of how you lead.

Pause, Reflect, and Apply

- What difference would one of the three activities described in this section make on you and those you lead?

  _____

  _____

  _____

- What will you do to create a habit of service? Commit right now to using at least one of the three suggestions.

  _____

  _____

  _____

Making Time for Opportunities

You have to make time to serve. It is human nature to create overambitious and overscheduled days. If you fail to make the time to serve, you are going to fail to notice the opportunities to serve because you will be too busy. Block off time every day for service.

When I work with teams and leaders, I often ask them to create a plan to serve others. I provide them with a number of examples of service on teams and in organizations. They start by selecting someone to serve and then writing down what they specifically will do, when they will do it, and the impact it is going to make as a result. Planning forces you to start creating your service habit. To get a free copy of the Care to Lead Leader service plan template sent to you, along with all of the other free tools and templates in this book, go to www.doyoucaretolead.com/tools.

You might also consider planning a half-hour a day to walk around the office looking for opportunities to serve. One leader I know found a way to serve that most people of average height wouldn't. In his words, "My team works in an office where they are each in cubicles. These cubicles go through the entire office. Because of my height I often look over their cubicle walls to say hi or to speak with them. Normally once a month, or more often, I get Lysol wipes and wipe down the tops of their cubicles to get all the dust off. Sounds funny, but it has meant a lot to the team over the years."

Simple? Yes. But meaningful opportunities can be found everywhere when you make the time to find them.

Acts of Service

In the bestselling book *The Giving Tree* by Shel Silverstein, the story is told about a relationship of a young boy and a tree. Perhaps you have read it. The tree throughout the boy's life tries to selflessly do everything it possibly can to make the boy happy. She allows the child to climb and play on her, swing from her branches, and even to pick and eat her apples. The boy visits the tree every day. He loves the tree and the tree loves him and is very happy.

As the boy grows older, he spends less and less time with the tree except for making time for things such as bringing his girlfriend to the tree and carving their initials into its trunk. Later as the boy becomes a man, he comes to the tree for material things as needed. She is able to provide for him things such as apples to sell for money and wood to help build a home and a boat. The tree remains happy by being able to continue to serve him.

In the final sad stages of the tree's life, it is but a stump. The boy, now an elderly man, pays the tree a visit. The tree is sad because it doesn't think it has anything else to offer. The now elderly man says that all he needs is a place to sit down and rest. The tree is happy to provide a stump. The man is then able to use the tree to sit and rest.

What this story demonstrates to me is the many and creative ways there are to selflessly serve. I have always loved seeing leaders find ways to serve: a fast food manager stepping up and taking over a cash register to help a busy team, a grocery manager stepping in to bag some groceries when seeing a checker who needs help, a leader staying late into the evening working with an employee to meet a project deadline. I have been the benefactor of such service myself.

Early in my career I was fortunate enough to have the most caring and thoughtful boss on the planet. At the time I was working on a training program that was due the next morning. Most managers would have said *adios, goodnight, see you in the morning* as they went home for the evening. But that wasn't who this leader was. Instead he asked me what I would like for dinner, ate with me, and then stayed with me until 5:30 the next morning!

That was over 20 years ago, and I still remember just about every detail of his kindness that evening. But this wasn't just a one-time thing with this thoughtful leader; he was regularly thinking about others. It was through his consistent and day-to-day acts of service that made the real impact on others. It was his sincere and specific compliments, cards with personal notes, and a willingness to be there and do anything he could to help that made the biggest difference. We don't forget those who deeply care about us.

Motivational author and speaker Simon Sinek dished out wise advice on love in an interview with Tom Bilyeu in 2017. In that interview he said, "She didn't fall in love with you because you remembered her birthday and brought her flowers on Valentine's Day. She fell in love with you because when you woke up in the morning, you said good morning to her before you checked your phone."[10] What Sinek was saying is that she fell in love with you because of the selfless and **consistent** acts of service over time, not because of some huge, once-in-a-while, grand and romantic gesture.

You won't make as strong of a connection with those you lead by doing only a once-a-year birthday celebration or an occasional team dinner. Although those acts of service are meaningful, they aren't enough. It's through the consistent selfless service, day in and day out, that really says, "I care." It's the wiping down the top of your teams' cubicles with Lysol. It's taking a package to the mail department or post office for a busy member of your team. It's shoveling the entrance to your building so others are safe. It's having sand-wiches delivered to the team so they don't have to go out in a bad snowstorm. It's showing up for a couple of hours to help someone on your team move. It's bringing in a mobile car wash service to wash your teams' cars in the parking lot. *Okay, that last one is a big one, but I think it is cool!* It's also as simple as giving a smile, holding the door open for someone, saying a kind word, and saying hello. It's doing these types of things day in and day out that make a difference in your leadership.

There are lots of opportunities to thoughtfully find meaningful ways to help others. The list of ideas we could come up if we were all in a room together is limitless.

However, I know what you might be thinking at this point: "How do I do all the things I have to do if I am serving as often as you are suggesting, Michael?" That is a fair question. However, service is never about the number of times, and I never said it was. It's not about serving 10 times, five times, or even one time a day. It's about consistency, not irresponsibility. It's about regularly doing the right thing at the right time for the right person.

Service is a priority with Care to Lead Leaders, but, of course, it isn't the only priority that leaders have. When service becomes a habit, you simply and consistently look for those little things (occasionally big things) that are most meaningful to those you lead in that moment. In the end, it's not as much or as hard as you think. And as you create a culture of service on your team(s) and organization(s), you aren't the only one generating good feelings and connections; the entire team and organization eventually is as well. It's not just your opportunity, but an opportunity for your entire team(s) and organizations too. But, as is the case with many of things I talk about in this book, again, it starts with you.

Service Impacts

Few have ever heard of Nicholas Winton. He was a humble man with a huge accomplishment that wouldn't be recognized by the world until 50 years after the fact.

Mr. Winton was a London stockbroker, and in December 1938, he was looking forward to a Swiss skiing vacation when a friend asked him to forgo his planned trip and visit him in Czechoslovakia to rescue Jewish children. At that time, Britain had a program called *Kindertransport,* which sent representatives to Germany and Austria to rescue Jewish children, saving 10,000 before World War II started.

In Czechoslovakia, however, there was no such mass effort for rescuing Jewish children. So, in response to this lack of effort, Winton got to work and created his own rescue program. It involved a great deal of time, work, ingenuity, and courage to accomplish.

The *New York Times*'s obituary of Nicholas Winton read, "[Winton's rescue efforts] involved dangers, bribes, forgery, secret contacts with the Gestapo, nine railroad trains, an avalanche of paperwork and a lot of money. Nazi agents started following him."[11]

Through his selfless courageous efforts, Nicholas Winton saved a total of 669 children from the Holocaust. To this day, these children call themselves "Winton's children."

Knighted by Queen Elizabeth II in 2003, Sir Nicholas Winton was a hero. Not many knew of Winton, and even fewer knew of the breadth of his accomplishments. His wife wasn't even aware of the extent of his heroism, that is, until 1988 when she found an old scrapbook in the attic containing the names of the children he rescued, their parents' names, and the names and addresses of the host families.

When Winton's wife brought the scrapbook to his attention, Winton suggested she throw it out, thinking it had no value. Of course, she didn't. Instead, she gave the scrapbook to a Holocaust historian. In that same year, 1988, the world also came to know this great humble servant and leader through a BBC television program titled "That's Life!" Winton was honored and was a member of the audience during the broadcast. The television host pointed out that he was sitting next to one of the children whom he rescued. The greeting was emotional as Winton wiped away tears, and the survivor expressed her heartfelt gratitude to this quiet hero. The host then asked if there was anyone else in the audience that night who owed their life to Nicolas Winton and if so, could they stand. Almost the entire audience stood. Winton slowly turned around to look and was overcome by emotion and tearfully touched by the moving surprise of so many that owed their life to him.

No one needed to ask Sir Nicholas Winton to take action. He saw a problem and found a way to use his talents and skills to serve and bless the lives of hundreds. That's what Care to Lead Leaders do. That's what you can do, too. This humble leader had no idea of the impact he had made on so many. You won't completely understand the impact you are having and will have as you humbly serve. But you are having an impact. Service changes those you lead. So, serve.

Serve First, Lead Second

In my first book, *You Are the Team: 6 Simple Ways Teammates Can Go from Good to Great,* I shared that, "At the heart of a successful team, you will find the selfless and caring hearts of its members." However, if we were to go deeper you would find that at the heart of every successful team is the heart of a selfless and caring leader.

It's easy to lead when others know that you care about them because of the ways you actively demonstrate it. Previously I said that service was the key to unlocking your leadership and the quickest way to establishing yourself as a leader by connecting. Make the choice to selflessly serve first and leading easily follows.

Care to Lead Leader Service Takeaways

- *Ubuntu* is everything that a leader should aspire to practice, to be, and to create.

- Service is the quickest way to unlocking leadership.

- Service changes hearts, and changed hearts change people, teams, and organizations.

- Service starts with you and ripples into teams and organizations because of connection, reciprocity, and multiplicity (the service effect).

- Creating a habit of service is about having the right heart, an awareness, physical reminders, and making the time.

- Service is not just your opportunity, but an opportunity for your entire team and organization.

- You won't ever completely understand the full effect your service is making on those you lead, but it is having an impact.

- Serve first and leading easily follows.

Notes

1. Desmond Tutu, "Mission and Philosophy," *Desmond Tutu Peace Foundation*, http://www.tutufoundationusa.org/desmond-tutu-peace-foundation/.

2. Ekaterina Walter, "In One Plane Ride, the Co-Founder of Southwest Airlines Teaches Us a Powerful Lesson," *Inc.*, Last modified June 8, 2017, https://www.inc.com/ekaterina-walter/a-simple-but-powerful-leadership-lesson-from-the-co-founder-of-southwest-airline.html.

3. Bill Dolack, "Heroism, Compassion, and Reconciliation by the Angel of Marye's Heights," *Christian History Society of America*, Last modified August 13, 2019, https://www.christianhistorysociety.com/kirkland.html.

4. David J. B. Trim, ed., *The Chivalric Ethos and the Development of Military Professionalism* (Leiden, the Netherlands: Brill, 2003), 342.

5. Ed Frauenheim, "Why Companies That Give Back Also Receive," *Fortune*, Last modified February 9, 2018, https://fortune.com/2018/02/09/bank-of-america-giving-back/.

6. Teresa Zabala, "Religious Panhandlers Are Provoking Anger at Airports," *New York Times*, December 22, 1967, 31.

7. Lionel Tiger and Robin Fox, *The Imperial Animal* (Piscataway, NJ: Transaction Publishers, 1997).

8. Amy Rees Anderson, "Can Compassion Contribute to Success?," *Forbes*, Last modified December 6, 2015, https://www.forbes.com/sites/amyanderson/2015/12/06/can-compassion-contribute-to-success/.

9. Darnell Mayberry, "Star Spangled Save: What Maurice Cheeks Did for Anthem Singer in Portland Is Still Remembered," *The Oklahoman*, Last modified April 13, 2010, https://oklahoman.com/article/3413717/star-spangled-save-what-maurice-cheeks-did-for-anthem-singer-in-portland-is-still-remembered.

10. Simon Sinek, "These Reactions to Simon Sinek Sharing Love Advice Will Give You All the Feels," *Goalcast*, Last modified February 13, 2018, https://www.goalcast.com/2018/02/13/simon-sinek-vaentines-day-love-advice/.

11. Robert D. McFadden, "Nicholas Winton, Rescuer of 669 Children from Holocaust, Dies at 106," *New York Times*, July 1, 2015, A1.

Chapter 2

Open (Up)

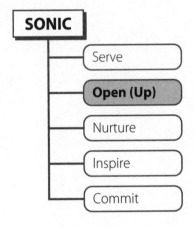

Creating more openness on your team starts with you opening up to your team.

Once you begin to serve those you lead thoughtfully, regularly, and compassionately, being able to get people to believe and follow you becomes a lot easier. The formula is now ready to start mixing; you just need the next ingredient—the willingness of you to be open and then creating a climate where people feel like they can safely open up and take risks.

Safety First

Charles Duhigg, a Pulitzer-award-winning journalist and author, wrote an extensive article in the *New York Times Magazine* about a massive investment and effort that Google undertook in 2012 titled "Project Aristotle."[1] The tech giant wanted to find out what was behind teams that were effective and others that were not. Google statisticians, researchers, sociologists, psychologists, engineers, and others gathered and deciphered data from hundreds of the company's teams trying to find out why some fell below expectations and others exceeded them.

What the Project Aristotle team discovered were five specific things that made the biggest difference on effective teams, with psychological safety being by far the most important of all of them. Amy Edmondson, a Harvard business professor, explained psychological safety as "a belief that one will not be punished or humiliated for speaking up with ideas, questions, concerns, or mistakes."[2] Psychological safety creates less focus on self-protection and a bigger focus from team members on the team's direction. Feeling safe to open up creates greater efficiencies and overall stronger teamwork.

As a grad student at Harvard years before, Edmundson was studying medical teams at hospitals in order to find out what distinguished the best-performing groups from others, much like what Google did later. She assumed she'd find that the top teams made the fewest medication errors. To her surprise, however, she found exactly the opposite. Better-performing teams seemed to be making more errors than worse-performing teams.

Later she learned though that the best teams weren't actually making more errors than the worse-performing teams, they were simply more open to admitting errors and discussing them more often. What actually distinguished the best-performing teams from the poor-performing teams was psychological safety.

It has been my experience with the many teams I have worked with over the years that those teams where members felt safe were at a very different level of performance than teams that didn't feel such safety. Because team members felt safe, they could be open, completely honest, passionately disagree with ideas and each other, and they were more likely to be accountable and hold each other accountable. Their interactions and meetings looked very different. Those types of teams to me felt like a functional family because of their ability to be so open with each other. They were safe but also very productive. They also learned by their mistakes quicker and prevented their teams and companies from losing face and losing money because they weren't afraid to speak up, raise issues, address concerns, suggest better ideas, and so on. Creating a climate where people feel safe starts with your willingness as a Care to Lead Leader to open up and to be vulnerable at times.

Opening Up

Matt Sakaguchi was a mid-level manager at Google at the time that Project Aristotle began. He was interested in the project because the last team he led didn't work very well together and he wanted to make sure things went better this time with his new team. He asked Project Aristotle researchers if they could help and they provided him with a survey for his team that he then administered. Sakaguchi thought he had a pretty strong team, but to his surprise when the results came back there were some glaring weaknesses.

Sakaguchi decided to bring his team together for an off-site meeting to talk about the survey results. But he started the meeting first by asking each team member to draw his or her life journey and how he or she got there that day. Sakaguchi went first and showed the team his journey and shared something he was fairly certain no one knew about: he had stage four cancer. His team was stunned; they didn't know what to say.

In the short 10 months that they had been working together, they came to like Sakaguchi. No one on the team had any idea that he had been dealing with this. Journalist Charles Duhigg explains what happened next. "After Sakaguchi spoke, another teammate stood and described some health issues of her own. Then another discussed a difficult breakup. Eventually, the team shifted its focus to the survey. They found it easier to speak honestly about the things that had been bothering them, their small frictions and everyday annoyances."[3]

Sakaguchi later said of the team activity in an interview with Massey Morris, manager of digital and marketing at Tory Burch:

> My goal with that exercise was to see that once you hear what people have gone through, you can never look at them the same. You start seeing them as people first, not a co-worker who is making your job harder. At this new level of sharing, we were actually able to get some discussions going about how we can work better as a team. After about a month, the dynamics of the team had changed and it became one of the best teams I've ever worked with at Google.[4]

Having an open team feels safer and makes everything better. Care to Lead Leaders recognize that power and do everything they can to create such a team or teams.

You Go First

Creating a place where people felt safe started with Matt Sakaguchi and his willingness to be open, which gave the green light for others to open up as well. And it starts with you, too.

Years ago, I was doing some consulting and development with a senior leadership team. At the time, they were having what seemed to be unrepairable issues. They didn't like each other and there had been a lot of unhealthy conflict, huge communication issues, and trust was at an all-time low. People were closed off and very little collaboration was happening. And as is usually the case, these problems cascaded down the entire organization affecting the morale of everyone.

I brought the team together to do a two-day intensive workshop on trust. Kicking the meeting off with an exercise, members of the team were asked to share a personal challenge that they had dealt with as a child. They were encouraged to be as vulnerable as they were comfortable being. I knew that the sharing had to start with the CEO, whom I will refer to as Scott (not his real name, of course).

Scott was perceived to be very closed. He was mostly about business and rarely took the time to get to know others on a more personal level. To be honest, most of the struggles with this company were due to his lack of leadership and trust in him as a leader. I had a direct and honest conversation with him before the meeting. Fortunately, at that point he was open to anything because his company was tanking fast.

I asked Scott if he would be willing in the kickoff exercise to share first. His openness was going to set the tone.

Based on my experience with teams and much like the experience that Sakaguchi's had at Google, I knew that if this leader could be open, others would be willing to be open as well, and openness was what this team needed to start getting back on track.

What happened next surprised me and completely shocked this entire leadership team. Scott went first as planned. He shared his experience of growing up with an alcoholic father. Here's the thing though: every member of that team knew who Scott's father was, which made it even more personal. His father had stopped drinking years ago, but the affect it had on Scott growing up was still very real. I assumed he had permission from his father to share his story.

Scott emotionally (and I am talking about weeping at times) shared how his father was rarely present, how as a young boy he never felt like he mattered much, and how he could never live up to his father's expectations. By the time he was done, he had every person in that room in tears, including myself. For the rest of the exercise each member of that team openly shared, and many times very emotionally shared, their greatest challenges growing up. After the exercise was over the team was in a very different place than they had ever been. The feeling in that conference room dramatically changed from what it was before we started. And the next two days were amazing as openness increased and trust, communication, and accountability improved, which all allowed for more open discussions on what was happening to the organization and how to fix it. That team forever changed from that point on.

Is this an extreme example of a leader being open? Yes, but it worked! Although I don't think it is always necessary for leaders to open up to the level that this leader did, opening up at some level begins to create higher levels of trust and safety and makes team members feel that they can be open as well. Creating more openness on your team starts with you opening up to your team. People want to follow a leader who is open, real, and human, not closed, fake, or perfect.

However, I feel at this point I should give a warning before going any further. Opening up doesn't mean sharing every day every single personal challenge you are having. It doesn't mean shouting every **single** little mistake you make, and in general letting people know you can't do your job—that is a lack of competence, not vulnerability. It also doesn't mean opening up about personal gripes you have with team members, your boss, other leaders, or even clients. It shouldn't feel to your team like complaining, being negative, or even critical. It also doesn't mean you share things you have no right sharing. Opening up in the wrong ways about the wrong things puts you at risk of undermining your own leadership. People may see you as weaker, not humble and open. There is a balance and that balance requires careful thought and good timing.

However, you have probably had a past leader who never opened up and showed any type of vulnerability, was always right and never wrong, "never made a mistake," never said he or she was sorry, and never asked for help or feedback. How did you feel about that leader? How safe did you feel opening up and expressing honest opinions, feedback, or concerns?

No One Is Perfect

Your ability as a Care to Lead Leader to humbly open up at appropriate times and be seen as human is critical to creating safety and trust on your team and in your organization.

Admit an "Oops"

On June 2, 2010, Armando Galarraga, a pitcher for the Detroit Tigers, was one out from pitching a perfect game, something that is rare in Major League Baseball. Pitching a perfect game means that in a complete game, at least nine innings, not a single opposing player gets on base. However, on the last out of the ninth inning, the first base umpire, Jim Joyce, ruled the runner safe and put an end to Galarraga's quest for a perfect game.

Joyce believed that he made the right call, that is, until he saw the replay for himself after the game. The replay showed that the runner was clearly out and that Galarraga should have gotten credit for a perfect game. The humble umpire tearfully and immediately went to the 28-year-old pitcher from Venezuela and apologized for getting the call wrong.

What happened next is just as great! Galarraga turned around and forgave Joyce for blowing a call that cost him something he may never do in his career again: throw a perfect game. "He probably feels more bad than me," Galarraga said. "Nobody's perfect. Everybody's human. I understand. I give the guy a lot of credit for saying, 'I need to talk to you.' You don't see an umpire tell you that after a game. I gave him a hug."[5]

We are often touched by people, like umpire Jim Joyce, who are humble enough and willing to admit a mistake, even at the risk of a lot of embarrassment. Leaders have opportunities to soften the hearts of those they lead and create teams where people feel safe to admit their own mistakes by admitting when they are in error. Shrugging it off, or acting like nothing happened, or even worse—denying it was a mistake makes it more likely others won't ever feel safe in admitting their mistakes. Hiding mistakes by team members can have huge negative effects downstream.

It is hard for many of us to admit our mistakes. By admitting a mistake, we might believe that others will see us as incapable or less intelligent. This is a terrifying thought for some leaders; however, none of it is true. When we admit our mistakes, we are often seen as more capable, intelligent, and even more credible. People relate to and are more connected to people who seem more human.

In the 1980s, there was a group of researchers at Cleveland State University that made an unexpected discovery. In an experiment, these researchers created two fictitious job applicants, David and John. Both applicants had identical résumés and letters of recommendation; however, in John's letters, there was the sentence, "Sometimes, John can be difficult to get along with." Both résumés were shown to several human resources directors. Which applicant do you suppose the directors preferred? Surprisingly the majority of them chose difficult-to-get-along-with John.[6]

It was concluded that the criticism of John made the praise of him more believable. Admitting John's weaknesses actually helped sell him. In short, admitting your flaws gives you more credibility! The more you are willing to admit your mistakes and take full responsibility for your actions, the more

61
Open (Up)

believable you will be. Humbleness does pay, if you give it a chance.

Members of your team(s) and in your organization(s) are going to make mistakes as well. Giving them permission to make mistakes and even to fail is part of creating a safe climate of openness on your team. After all, no one is perfect, and the way you facilitate how failure is viewed can make a big difference to individuals, teams, and an organization's overall success.

American billionaire and founder and CEO of Spanx, Sara Blakely, was taught to embrace failure as an important means of learning as a child. She incorporated this into her culture at Spanx as well. In a video by *Business Insider,* Blakely shares how her father would actually high-five her and congratulate her at the dinner table if she shared a failure she had that week. She said, "he'd actually be disappointed if I didn't have something that I'd failed at that week."[7] These experiences in her words "reframed" her definition of failure.

How you respond to others when they make a mistake matters. Most everything we learn in life requires some kind of failure: from potty training, to riding a bike, to learning a new software system, to taking the lead for the first time on a project. Each is filled potentially with errors, mistakes, not to mention frustration. The only way not to fail is to not try in the first place. How you respond to mistakes and failure in your own life, which is often heavily influenced by how others respond to you, has an impact on how you learn, to what level you learn, and how confident and willing you are to take risks in the future.

When you were learning to walk, you took a step and what happened? Everyone around you smiled, applauded, and encouraged you to keep trying, so you did. You took another step and either fell or were able to take one more step. What happened? You received more smiles and encouragement. At each step you adjusted something you did before and improved until not only were you walking but eventually started doing more and more complicated things like running, playing a sport, or maybe even walking across a tight rope! The point is, you improved because of how others reacted to you.

What would have happened if with your first step and fall your mother or father became angry and told you, you should haven't even tried and prevented you from trying again? When would you have eventually learned how to walk? Although this might seem like a silly example, it really isn't too far-fetched with how some leaders sabotage those they lead by making them not feel comfortable with failing.

In Blakely's company she has created what she calls, "the 'oops' of Spanx."[8] She said they encourage people to fail and that she brings up her failures all of the time. The "oops" of Spanx includes oops in its history and the oops that Blakely recently did. She has turned that into "oops meetings" where employees are encouraged to stand up and talk about their oops and mistakes. She says, "If you can create a culture where [your employees] are not terrified to fail or make a mistake, then they're going to be highly productive and more innovative."[9] Blakely should know!

Creating a work environment where people can easily admit mistakes speeds up the learning curve for everyone, creates greater efficiencies, and avoids bigger and more costly errors later. And open leaders are seen as more authentic, connect more easily, and inspire more often. They are also seen as more caring.

Pause, Reflect, and Apply

- How do you react to the mistakes of those you lead? What might you change?

  _____

  _____

  _____

- How comfortable are you at showing your "oops" moments with others? How can you get more comfortable?

  _____

  _____

  _____

- What are some specific ways that you can begin to show your less-than-perfect side and encourage others to show theirs?

  _____

  _____

  _____

Say You Are Sorry

Part of admitting a mistake sometimes includes saying you are sorry, or "I apologize." Being able to say you are sorry requires open humility. It's not only admitting that you made a mistake but also acknowledging that people were hurt by your mistake. Saying sorry is about taking accountability for what you did and whom you affected by what you did. And it creates an openness on your part that helps those you lead feel safer.

How would you feel about a leader who made a mistake that affected you and who later looked you straight in the eyes and with all of his heart said, "I am sorry"? The chances are that you have rarely had that happen to you. I can probably count on three and a half fingers (the half being a "kind of sorry") the times it happened to me over my long career. But you have an opportunity to be different, to be more open than that. You can be a Care to Lead Leader who cares enough about those you lead so that when you make a mistake, and someone is affected by that mistake, you immediately and sincerely apologize. Leaders who are open enough to apologize create a safety of openness on their teams.

Pause, Reflect, and Apply

- When was the last time you made a mistake and said you were sorry? Did you take **full accountability** for the mistake? How sincere was your apology? What would you change, if anything?

  _____

  _____

  _____

Ask for Help

Care to Lead Leaders ask for help; weak leaders don't. Weak leaders fear that they might be seen as less than capable (which is an overall theme with less-than-open leaders). Care to Lead Leaders know that asking for help is an opportunity for the team to feel valued, and it sets a tone of creating a culture of helpfulness.

All leaders must recognize that they have limitations and that asking for help moves them past those limitations. They are not only modeling for their teams what humbleness can do but also by opening up and asking for help, leaders are giving permission to their team(s) and organization(s) to do the same. Asking for help also opens the door for service. Others need the opportunity to serve you, which generates good feelings across the team.

Pause, Reflect, and Apply

- When is the last time you couldn't do something for whatever reason and asked for help from someone on the team you lead? What will you change when it comes to asking for help in the future? How can you help your team feel more comfortable asking for help?

  _____

  _____

  _____

Ask for Input

Asking those you lead for input from time to time also creates a climate of openness. How can someone you lead not feel valued and as a result open up to you when you ask, "Carrie, you always have great ideas; can you tell me how you feel things are going?" Or, "Tyler, I value your opinion and would like to get your input on how we can do this better next time." When people know you value them and genuinely want their input, they are more likely to feel safe and open up.

Pause, Reflect, and Apply

- What is something you can ask for input on right now? Who will you ask? Why will you ask that person? What impact is it going to make on that person and on your team?

  _____

  _____

  _____

Ask for Feedback

Have you ever had someone give you negative feedback and you cringed, wanted to get away, became upset, maybe angry, and even started having a strong dislike for the person who gave you the feedback? If you have, you aren't outside of the norm. Most people when they receive feedback initially struggle. Why? A lot of it has to do with our fight-or-flight mode of survival. Psychologists and neurobiologists have studied this and found that our brains react much quicker to negative stimuli because of the way they are wired, and when we get such stimuli, we either want to run away or rumble.

But as you know, feedback is powerful, and when you embrace it for what it is, it can change who you are. However, those you lead can struggle in providing it. VitalSmarts, a leadership training company, conducted an online survey to understand how comfortable employees were in sharing critical feedback with their managers. Eighty percent of 1,335 respondents said that everyone knows about and even talks about a significant weakness their boss has but never speaks directly to their manager about it.[10] In other words, most of those you lead aren't going to come to you and provide helpful and possibly game-changing feedback unless you regularly seek it.

In the past when I was conducting one-on-ones with those I led, I always ended our meeting by asking, "What can I do to improve as a leader?" I realized that I was opening myself up, but I also understood that if the people I led would be honest with me, and I would work on getting better based on what I was hearing, I could improve dramatically as their leader.

Initially those I asked would say something like, "I can't think of anything right now." But I knew that wasn't true; there was something I could do better. Each meeting I would continue to ask the same thing and get the same answer. It wasn't until I started pointing out things in these meetings that I believed I could do better that they started opening up, by first agreeing with me and then suggesting things to me. And once I started asking for honest feedback on how I had improved on what I was hearing from them, each month I kept getting more and more additional feedback on how I could be a better leader. Is this hard? Absolutely! But do you care enough to ask? That's the question.

If you could push a button and magically have an objective detailed list of things you could start improving on immediately as a leader, would you push it? I believe most of us would. Care to Lead Leaders care enough to openly ask those they lead for that list.

When you are receiving feedback and doing something with that feedback to get better, those around you take notice. Because you are open, again, others feel like they can be open. Because they realize that you don't see yourself as perfect, they don't believe they are either. As a result, everyone becomes more open to trying to be better together. That's how it works!

Pause, Reflect, and Apply

- Have you ever asked for feedback on how you are doing as a leader from those you lead? How often do you ask? Is there anything you will change?

  _____

  _____

  _____

- What can you specifically start doing to make your team feel more comfortable in giving you honest feedback?

  _____

  _____

  _____

- Set some time aside each meeting you have with those you lead to ask what you can do better. Take notes and regularly update them on what you are specifically doing to improve.

  _____

  _____

  _____

Norms to Perform

Team norms are a powerful Care to Lead Leader tool. In fact, you can't create a highly safe climate of openness without them. They are a set of guidelines that a team establishes together that safely support the interaction of team members. Norms give members of your team permission and a feeling of safety to be open and to embrace others' openness.

"He consistently interrupts, talks over people, can't shut up, and I get very little participation in my meetings from others as a result." Those were the frustrations described to me by Stephanie, a leader who was at her wit's end and had no idea how to fix the rude and monopolizing behavior of one of her team members, Jeff. I asked her if she had talked to him, she said she had several times but to no avail. I asked if she had any types of team norms in place. At that time, she didn't.

I suggested that Stephanie quickly set some norms with her team. Naturally, with the team very aware of Jeff's monopolizing behavior and with her leadership guidance, they could easily create a norm that included not interrupting and talking over another person. Once the team's five to seven (I highly recommend not setting more than seven because if everything is important, then nothing is important) norms were in place, Stephanie would then challenge the team to abide by the norms and commit them to heart by the next meeting. I also asked Stephanie to bring a bell for each team member to the next meeting. She looked at me a little funny, but as I explained to her, the bells were a fun way to bring attention to any violation of a norm. In fact, I suggested that Stephanie purposely violate a norm at the start of the meeting and have several on the team who were asked ahead of time to ring bells when she did.

As the meeting began, Stephanie indeed purposefully violated a norm. The two people she asked previous to the meeting to ring their bells rang them quickly and loudly and thereafter the rest of the team rang theirs as well. They all laughed and Stephanie apologized and said she would work on it. After that, any violation of a norm, including interrupting and talking over others, was immediately followed by bells, lots of laughter, and apologies. Jeff's tendency to interrupt and talk over others lessened substantially and participation in meetings increased and eventually included everyone.

What I did was help this team set a group of norms to improve good team behavior and create a safe climate of openness. You can effectively use these tools with your team(s) as well.

Norms can be set for many things such as being on time to meetings, being prepared for meetings, agreeing how quickly people answer their phones or return an email, creating a no cell phone or technology policy during meetings, doing what you say you will do, and so on. But some of the most important and powerful norms set on teams are those concerning openness:

- Treating each other with kindness and respect
- Giving others the benefit of the doubt
- Listening to understand first
- Openly admitting mistakes
- Not throwing people under the bus
- Avoiding politics
- Having permission to be genuine and open about ideas
- Respectfully challenging someone if you don't agree
- Supporting each other as needed
- Establishing that it's okay to not have all the answers

There are many other team norms that could be listed here, but the important thing is that you create these as a team. The goal of setting up such norms is to create a safe place where people can feel open in; take risks; express how they feel; respectfully but passionately (if necessary) disagree; provide bold, direct, and honest feedback; courageously contribute ideas; admit when a mistake is made; or ask for help.

Would you agree that if your people felt safe with even just a few of these actions that it would make a difference? Team norms are an important tool that you can't afford not to use in your leadership in order to create openness.

Pause, Reflect, and Apply

- Do you currently have a formal set of team norms? If yes, what kind of difference are they making? Is there anything you need to adjust or restart?

  _____

  _____

  _____

- If your team doesn't currently have a set of team norms, set some time in your next meeting and begin to discuss. Use some of the given examples and begin to brainstorm norms and work it down to five to seven that the team can agree with and then start using them.

  _____

  _____

  _____

- Put your team's norms at the top of every meeting agenda. About once or twice a month review the norms with your team and talk about how you are doing together with each of them.

  _____

  _____

  _____

Support, Encourage, and Mine

If a gardener fails to give a plant water, fertilizer, weed around it, and protect it early on from wind and frost, it won't ever reach its full potential and may not even grow at all and instead die. Similar to a plant, if you set up norms, for example, but fail to regularly support, encourage, and mine them early on, those norms will fail to be adopted and embraced. In turn you are not going to be successful in creating a team where others feel as safe. Creating a climate of safety is an active and proactive activity.

Support and Encourage

Creating teams where people can open up requires regular support and encouragement. Care to Lead Leaders ask from time to time how safe those they lead feel in opening up. They ask them what they can do to improve more openness and what they can do to help them feel safer.

As it pertains to norms, with the leaders help, the team regularly asks, How are we doing? Where have we improved? How can we improve more? What gets measured has the opportunity to get better. Again, as already mentioned, I would highly suggest that you put your team norms somewhere on every team meeting agenda as a reminder to review, measure, and discuss periodically.

Also important is that you positively point out behaviors that support openness and team norms both when your team is meeting and in one-on-one settings. In team meetings, for example, when someone takes a risk with a suggested idea, let that person know that you appreciate their risk and idea.

If taking the risk aligns with team norms, then point that out as well. The more you support and encourage openness, the more willing people will be to practice openness, and eventually the safer everyone will start to feel in being open. Openness needs to be massaged, supported, and encouraged.

Pause, Reflect, and Apply

- Add an agenda item at your next one-on-one meeting with those you lead titled *safety discussion*. Ask them how safe they feel in being open, what you can do to help them, and what you can do to create a greater climate of safety going forward.

  _____

  _____

  _____

- Start becoming more aware of opportunities to positively point out strong openness behaviors both individually and in team meetings.

  _____

  _____

  _____

Mine

A quick tool to help you create openness is to mine for it. Mining is a proactive approach to creating openness. If someone in a meeting, for example, is being quiet and his body language shows that he isn't comfortable with something being said, a leader or a teammate might ask him what he is thinking, or why it feels and seems like he doesn't agree. Teams consist of many differing personalities and some need a little more prodding than others to be open. It might be at the moment that he just doesn't feel safe. But the leader's and team's support and encouragement can help. Of course, be careful not to push too hard; that person might close even more. But with the right norms and team culture, mining can be effective for all.

Pause, Reflect, and Apply

- What would mining look like on your team? What can you do to do more of it as it relates to creating greater openness? What are some of the things you have to be cautious of as it pertains to mining on your team?

_____

_____

_____

Care to Lead Leader Open (Up) Takeaways

- What distinguishes the best-performing teams from the poorest-performing teams is a climate in which people feel safe in being open.

- Creating more openness on your team starts with you opening up to your team.

- When you are willing to admit mistakes, you are often seen as more capable, intelligent, and even more credible. People relate to and are more connected to people who seem more human.

- Admitting mistakes, saying you are sorry, asking for help, asking for input, and asking for feedback not only improves your relationships with those you lead but also gives permission for others to humbly do the same.

- Team norms give those you lead permission to take risks and respectfully express how they feel; to passionately disagree; to provide bold, direct, and honest feedback; and to courageously contribute ideas.

- Supporting, encouraging, and mining ensures that openness is embraced and adopted by those you lead.

Notes

1. Charles Duhigg, "What Google Learned from Its Quest to Build the Perfect Team," *New York Times Sunday Magazine,* February 27, 2016, 20.
2. Amy Edmondson, "Building a Psychologically Safe Workplace," *Ted: Ideas Worth Spreading,* Video File, May 4, 2014, https://www.youtube.com/watch?v=LhoLuui9gX8.

3. Charles Duhigg, "What Google Learned from Its Quest to Build the Perfect Team."

4. Massey Morris, "This Google Manager Shares His Secrets for Building an Effective Team," *Fast Company,* Last modified August 15, 2018, https://www.fastcompany .com/90218743/this-google-manager-shares-his-secrets-for-building-an-effective-team.

5. Paul White, "Missed Call Leaves Detroit's Armando Galarraga One Out Shy of a Perfect Game" *USA Today,* June 2, 2010.

6. Harry Beckwith, *Selling the Invisible: A Field Guide to Modern Marketing* (New York: Warner Books, 1997), 157.

7. Sara Blakely, "Spanx CEO Sara Blakely Offers Advice to Redefine Failure." *Business Insider,* Video File, September 8, 2016, https://www.youtube.com/watch?v=OZEPbyIA8XI.

8. Ibid.

9. Blaire Briody, "Sara Blakely: Start Small, Think Big, Scale Fast," *Insights by Stanford Business,* Last modified June 21, 2018, https://www.gsb.stanford.edu/insights/sara-blakely-start-small-think-big-scale-fast.

10. Joseph Grenny and Brittney Maxfield, "How Leaders Can Ask for the Feedback No One Wants to Give Them," *Harvard Business Review,* Last modified July 29, 2019, https://hbr.org/2019/07/how-leaders-can-ask-for-the-feedback-no-one-wants-to-give-them.

Chapter 3

Nurture

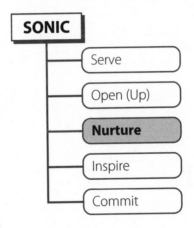

When leadership is personal, people will respond in deep and personal ways.

A farmer and his workers had just finished harvesting a full truckload of sugar beets. The route to the refinery was a bumpy dirt road. While making the journey some of the beets fell off the truck. Most farmers would have continued the journey and not thought much about those that had fallen. However, this farmer was different.

He pulled over to the side of the road and instructed his workers to retrieve the fallen beets. They looked at him confused; so much work for so few beets. But this farmer explained to them that there was just as much sugar in most of those that had slipped as those that had remained.

Each beet on that truck and most every beet that had fallen from the truck had value. Your ultimate goal as a Care to Lead Leader is to find and tap into the value of every person you lead. This means you are helping them discover their unique gifts and talents and supporting, developing, and encouraging them to realize their full potential. Your people need you to deeply care, and you, your team, and the organization need what they provide. This is nurturing, the third part of the Care to Lead Leader Formula.

I have always loved the word *nurture* and its relation to leadership. Nurture by definition is the process of caring for and encouraging the growth or development of someone or something. In this case it is caring for and encouraging the growth and development of those you lead. It is a proactive selfless act of service, and it is what Care to Lead Leaders regularly think about and do.

But before we jump more into the how of nurturing, it is important that we take a look at what it isn't.

When Nurturing Takes a Wrong Turn

It's possible that when you think of helping others perform at their highest levels in the workplace, you think of performance management. And that makes sense ... sort of.

I have never liked the term *performance management*. It sounds cold and uninspiring. It creates some level of anxiety with employees and bosses alike. It conjures up feelings of processes and predictable outcomes that feel box-like or factory-focused. If employee A fails to do this, then do step B. Or, if Nancy does this, then give her warning number one. It sounds to me more like the subway ride that we discussed previously in the introduction than a rocket ride.

Although the process itself in theory makes sense, many times unfortunately it doesn't become what it is intended to be. This might have to do as much with the term and its emphasis on management as it has to do with the thing's leaders neglect or the wrong emphasis they put on it while "performance managing." Leaders who use performance management often miss a key component as well—that people are unique and they want to feel cared about.

A number of years ago I did some work with a manager of a fairly large organization. She loved performance management, but for all of the wrong reasons. She used it as a threat, not a development opportunity. At any given time, she had three to five of her staff members (and oftentimes more) on some kind of corrective action plan. Everything was black and white to her. If you did this, then you could expect this as a consequence—whether it was a reward or punishment.

Her approach might have worked with animal training, but it didn't work as well with people. She ended up firing a lot of employees. As a result, very few in her organizations trusted or liked her. Because of her focus on management, instead of leadership, people did just enough *not* to be negatively performance managed. It never felt like she cared about people; she was more focused on processes and results. She is what I call a *cookie cutter manager,* which is the antithesis of a nurturing leader.

Cookie Cutter Management

Cookie cutter management happens when a leader, such as in the previous example, looks at every individual and problem the same way. It fails to take into account the differences in people and the uniqueness of every situation. It is old school, and it never worked in leadership long ago and does not work today. Every person on your team comes to you with different experiences, histories, gifts and talents, skills and perspectives. What is right for one could very well not be right for another.

If you take an apple tree, for example, and plant it in the hot, low desert, you aren't going to get many apples. If you take an avocado tree and plant it in the mountains of Utah, you aren't going to get many avocados. But if you take each tree and plant them in the right climate, with the right amount of water, the correct mixture of soil, and provide it with the proper care, each will thrive. Those we lead are like trees. Each comes to us with different root structures, age, branches, leaf colors, and tolerances. Some are easily affected by one kind of pest, and others aren't affected at all. Some easily bend with the wind and others not so much. How we nurture trees or people is going to make a big impact on how they ultimately respond and thrive.

Leaders must move away from performance management and cookie cutter styles of management of approaching and solving every people problem the same way. They instead must move to a nurturing style of leadership (focus on leadership), in which people are individually and personally valued, cared about, grown, and rewarded. When leadership is personal, people will respond in deep and personal ways. Nurturing is how you deepen trust, create connection, dramatically improve engagement, and explode results!

Nurturing leaders have what Jack Welch, former CEO of General Electric, calls the *generosity gene*. Leaders who have this gene love to take care of their people, they get excited about seeing their employees succeed, it makes their day to give someone a promotion or a raise. The good news is that every leader has the capability of acquiring this gene. Nurturing leaders happen to have it already.

So, how do you become a more nurturing leader? How do you get the generosity gene? How do your people ultimately reap the benefits of your nurturing leadership? The answers to those questions are the focus of the rest of this chapter.

Move Up, Over, or Off

None of us are who we are today without nurturing. Someone at some point in our life invested in our growth. It could have been parents, a coach, a teacher, a boss ... someone cared about us and believed in us enough to help us see and reach our potential.

The process of nurturing for leaders is about understanding the uniqueness, talents, and value that everyone on your team brings. It is about having regular thoughts, feelings, and ideas about each person on your team and what you can do to help that person get on board, grow, and continue to grow. It is about helping people do things that they never thought they could do. It requires that you consistently think and put the needs of those you lead above everything else. Nurturing is at the heart of Care to Lead Leaders, and it requires your attentive focus on others' growth.

When it comes to growth, you have three choices as a leader: you can either move people up (to help them improve), over (to put them in another role or on a different team), or off (to remove them completely from your organization). The key is to be moving people in the best direction for them. It isn't always easy, but it's worth it.

Note: There is actually a fourth choice as well, but it isn't a choice for Care to Lead Leaders—and that's to do nothing. Doing nothing is what many leaders unfortunately choose to do. They don't want to have the difficult conversations because they are hard. They don't want to spend time understanding the unique history, challenges, and capabilities of each person they lead because "they don't have time." In other words, they fail to really care.

Out of the three choices of moving up, over, or off, the great majority of your time and focus must be spent on moving people up.

Move Up

The priority for any great leader is to move people up, not over or off. Having regular conversations, discovering strengths, identifying gaps, and developing people is what Care to Lead Leaders do to move those they lead up.

Every person you lead deserves a real effort from you in helping them grow. Unfortunately, very few leaders care enough to make the effort. When US employees were asked if their manager provided meaningful feedback, only 23% strongly agreed. When asked if someone at work encourages their development, only 30% strongly agreed. There are consequences. In that same study they found that the number one reason people leave jobs is due to a lack of development and career growth.[1] Yes, we have a problem, don't we? Nurturing people and helping them move up requires more than a rushed once-a-year conversation about their performance.

If you were coaching a high school, collegiate, or professional basketball team, it would be crazy to think that having a once-a-year or even a once-a-month coaching session with a player would be enough. You would be well on your way to a losing season if that were the case. Every basketball coach I have known at this level has spent time with players individually setting goals; encouraging them and giving careful instruction; correcting and praising them in drills, scrimmages, and games; regularly looking at their basketball stats to gauge their performance; and consistently finding unique ways to support, inspire, and motivate them. They know their players personally, they understand their capabilities, and they make finding ways to improve each of them a priority with the focus being on moving them up, not over or off.

Yes, there was a time that expectations were such that you simply told people what to do, and they did it without much dialog. You were just expected to get it done. But that has changed *for the good*. The expectations of employees now is that there are conversations between the leader and employee and that collaboration is the norm, not the rare exception. People want to feel like people. People want to be treated like people. People want to feel valued. They need leaders, not once-in-a-while managers.

So, how do you regularly nurture and focus on moving people up? You start by classifying where each employee is. On every team people usually fall into one of five groups— rock stars, rising stars, steady stars, falling stars, and deceiving stars.

Rock Stars We all love the rock stars on our teams. They are those people who not only do what they are asked but also many times don't even need to be asked. With a wealth of experience and unique skills, their contribution to the team is critical. Rock stars are the "get 'er done and then some" people on your team as it pertains to both effort and results. These stars have the best attitudes, are helpful, and are the team members who others seek first for their opinions and help. They are looked up to by members of your team and by others in the organization. People love to be around the rock stars.

Unfortunately, they can also be the most burnt-out members of your team. I want to shout out a warning: if you are regularly giving your rock stars the bulk of the most important work because they seem to be the only ones who can meet your expectations—eventually it won't matter how much you care, how many incentives and rewards you provide, or how valued they feel; they are going to eventually burn out and maybe even leave. This is one more reason you have to regularly nurture and focus on moving up every member of your team.

Second warning, don't neglect the rock stars in terms of nurturing; many leaders tend to do that a little. Just because they put a gold star on everything they do and knock it out of the park time after time, rock stars need nourishing as well. I have always loved the quote attributed to St. Jerome, "Good, better, best. Never let it rest. 'Til your good is better and your better is best." How much better does your team get when your rock stars are continuing to launch to places that no one else has seen before?

Take the time supporting, rewarding, and moving your rock stars up. Ask them how they feel about things, what you can do to ease their burdens, what they would like to be doing a year or two years from now, and how you can support them in getting there. Do everything in your power to remove obstacles and help them move way beyond where they are today. Their performance elevates everyone else's.

Rising Stars The only difference between your rising stars and your rock stars is their experience and opportunities for development. They haven't quite made it into the spotlight yet, but they are quickly on their way. When tasked with something, rising stars use every bit of experience (though limited) and creativity they have to exceed everyone's expectations.

Ensure you are giving your rising stars the tools, development, and experiences they need to become rock stars. Encourage them and let them know what potential you see in them. Similar with every star, provide them direct, bold, and honest feedback.

Steady Stars This group of people on your team could very well be called the *steady Eddies*. They consistently get done what they are tasked with doing, but not much more. They punch in the clock at 9 and are usually out by 5. They don't necessarily elevate the performance on your team, but they do what they are asked. You are going to see work that usually meets your expectations, but rarely exceeds.

Steady stars need lots of inspiring, frank conversations, encouragement, support, development, and challenges with clear expectations in order to start moving up to rock stars. When nurtured appropriately, many steady stars will start to thrive.

Falling Stars Falling stars aren't difficult to identify. They are the ones who tend to get very little done, seem unmotivated, and lack any desire to do anything extraordinary. They often drag their feet on things, miss deadlines, are often pretty negative, and do just enough not to get fired.

Every member of your team knows who the falling stars are, and they are watching to see what you do with them. How you work with your falling stars matters to you, your team, and the entire organization. Ignore them and you send your team a message. Nurture them and you send your team a message. There is significant meaning in both messages— I highly recommend sending them a message of nurturing.

Ignoring your falling stars tells your team, your larger organization, and even the falling stars themselves that you don't care. The unfortunate tendency of many leaders is to give falling stars less and less work to do and to continue to ignore their lack of quality and production, somehow thinking they will magically go away. After all, you need the best getting done what needs to get done in the best way. Instead of investing time in getting everyone better, these leaders invest in burdening rock stars and others with a portion of the falling stars' work. Hence, the burnout of a rock star (there's a title of a book somewhere in that).

However, Care to Lead Leaders understand that taking care of the bottom raises the top. Falling stars take a lot of attention and time, but nurturing them right from the start could save you a lot of time in the end.

Deceiving Stars Usually a strong but small minority on teams, deceiving stars need special mention because of the damage they potentially can do to your team(s) and organization(s). This group gets things done, but it is usually at the expense of relationships, team morale, and ultimately teamwork. Some leaders can be deceived by this group of stars and often consider them rock stars, instead of bottom stars. But beware! They are really bottom-tier falling stars, not rock stars.

In a wonderful Ted Talk titled "Forget the Pecking Order at Work," Margaret Heffernan, an entrepreneur and author, refers to what I am calling *deceiving stars* as *super chickens*. She shares an interesting experiment done by William Muir, an evolutionary biologist at Purdue University who was interested in productivity.

Muir chose to use chickens in his productivity experiment for one simple reason—you can easily measure a chicken's productivity by counting their eggs. His goal was to find out what factors could make one group of chickens more productive over another.

He broke his chickens into two groups. The first flock he selected were average chickens. He left this first flock alone for six generations. The second flock he chose only the best— this is the flock Heffernan called *super chickens*. And each successive generation he would continue to select only the best of the best of these super chickens for breeding, in hopes of creating what you might call super, super chickens.

After six generations with both flocks he found something very intriguing. The first flock of average chickens did just fine. They seemed happy, plump, had lots of feathers, and their egg production had increased dramatically.

What about the second flock? All but three of the super chickens were dead. Those three had pecked the others to death! These super chickens had only achieved their success and survived by suppressing the productivity of the rest.[2]

They were strong egg producers and performers, but at the expense of the rest of the flock or team. These are the rock stars on your team (high performers) who are really falling stars in rock star clothing. And although they may initially be viewed as rock stars, over time they wear everyone out, including leaders. Their only focus is on themselves and they do everything they can to put themselves in the spotlight. Hoarding information, taking all of the credit, or failing to pitch in when someone needs help are just a few of some of the unhealthy behaviors of deceiving stars.

Unfortunately, leaders often fail to do anything with these super chickens because they get so much done. But there is a problem, and it is a big, big problem. Treating deceiving stars as rock stars will begin to alienate your people, diminish team trust, lessen communication, and cause a whole host of relationship problems that will ultimately slow down your team. Selfishness on teams tends to do that.

The Practice of Moving Up You might have noticed that every categorization we just discussed has the word *star*. That's intentional. If someone isn't a star today, she has the potential with nurturing to become one tomorrow. Just like the beets that had fallen off the truck, the farmer believed most of them had just as much sugar potential as those that had remained. Even some of your falling and deceiving stars can rise with the right nurturing care.

So, what minimal level of performance do you accept as it pertains to rock stars, rising stars, steady stars, falling stars, and deceiving stars? When I ask this question, people often say rock star status, of course! However, most leaders accept far lower.

Pause, Reflect, and Apply

- Group those you lead into each of the categorizations of rock star, rising star, steady star, falling star, or deceiving star. You can download a free Care to Lead Leader Nurturing Grid for categorizing and taking action at www.doyoucaretolead .com/tools.

  _____

  _____

  _____

There is a good chance that if you categorized your people that they will fall into at least four of the five-star classifications, with a few possibly in the falling star and maybe even the deceiving star categories. If you only have people in the top two, then congratulations, you are doing a lot of things right. But if you have people you would put in the steady star or even the falling and deceiving star classifications, then this must be the level of performance you accept, right? Why else would they be there?

Care to Lead Leaders are only okay with rising star and rock star level performance. Through regularly nurturing, they do everything in their power to move every member of their team up to a higher classification, and if they can't, they move them over or off. Why? Because they care about the success of every person they lead. Care to Lead Leaders regularly ask the following types of questions every day with the focus on growing people up:

"Where specifically are Pam's gaps?"

"Does David require more coaching and attention?"

"Does Kristen need specific development in this area?"

"Is there a project that I can give Phil that would help him succeed at another level?"

"What is the difficult discussion I need to have with Pat?"

Pause, Reflect, and Apply

- What are you going to do to start moving every member of your team up? Create a plan of action for those you lead based on their classification. Plans should be created for every star, including rock stars. *Note: Your plan may also include moving people over or off—more on that later.* Again, you can download a free Care to Lead Leader Nurturing Grid for categorizing and taking action at: www.doyoucaretolead.com/tools.

  _____

  _____

  _____

It is important to point out that people can fluctuate between the categorizations in this grid. While someone might be a rock star today, they could become a steady star and even a falling star tomorrow and vice versa.

About 50% of the people you lead are going to be steady stars. On an average team, another 20% to 30% are going to be your rock stars and rising stars, and the other 20% to 30% will be your falling stars, mixed with a possible deceiving star or two.

I have seen this distribution with about every team that I have consulted with and developed, and when you focus on moving people up, you take everything up. Imagine for a minute leading an entire team of rock stars and rising stars. You would be spending your time on nurturing those who want to be nurtured and helping move up those who want to be moved up. As a result, you would see productivity, creativity, ideas, and focus improve dramatically and maybe even exponentially. What does that do for your team? What does that do for you? What are you going to do about it? Your goal has to be to move every member of your team to the rock star level, right?

The hard reality is, not everyone is going to be a fit on your team and what you are trying to do, no matter how much nurturing you do. Their behavior and performance level is going to always be subpar for some reason. Do you accept it, or do you do something about it? Leaders who deeply care about those they lead choose the latter. They do something about it because they care about doing what is best for the employee first as well as doing what is best for the team, organization, and company. And sometimes, the most difficult thing to do is the right thing to do for everyone. There are times you are going to have to fix the problem at the toughest of tough root levels.

Every summer for many years my boys have had the difficult chore of pulling weeds in the berry garden. If you know anything about berry gardens, you understand that it requires you to sit in the hot sun (or cool early morning—my sons never figured this one out) weeding inside and around the bushes and being extra careful so as not to be pricked by one of the many abundant thorns. Well, long story short, they hate this chore. So, one particular hot summer afternoon they had a "brilliant" idea. Instead of pulling the weeds from their roots, they would just simply throw as much dirt as they could over them.

The next day as I went out to water the garden; the weeds that they had thrown dirt over had magically popped up and appeared all over the garden again. They learned a lesson that day, you can't simply throw dirt over a weed and expect it to solve your problems. Likewise, leaders can't ignore and wish away poor behavior and performance. The weeds will always be there. The same problems will continue to resurface over and over again. You must care enough about those you lead to do the difficult thing and get a hold of the root, which could require moving people over or off.

Move Over
Some people are better suited in another seat on the bus then the one they are currently sitting in. When you care about every person you lead, you diligently find the best seat for

them. Maybe they have a unique skill that is better suited for another team. Maybe they would like their job better if they had y challenges instead of z challenges. Possibly they might just need a change in leadership.

Whichever seat you find for them, make sure it is a comfortable fit where they truly have the opportunity to thrive. Simply moving them somewhere else without giving it much thought usually means you are just taking yours and the team's problem and moving it to another leader and team. In the long run that is not fair to that employee, the new leader, and the new team. It's not what Care to Lead Leaders do.

If you find somewhere you think will be a good fit, then it is important to discuss it at length with potential leaders. Be open and honest and figure out how you can support and help this steady or falling star thrive.

Move Off

Nourishing those you lead can sometimes hurt. I loved watching the "Little Rascals" show on television growing up. For those of you not familiar with the Little Rascals, they were a group of fun and sometimes mischievous poor neighborhood children who were regularly coming up with creative ways to spend their days. I watched them every weekday after school as a child in Southern California in the 1970s. In fact, I organized and led my own Little Rascals gang!

One particular episode has stuck in my mind for years. Spanky, one of the main young characters, was about to be punished. Being fairly mischievous and pretty smart, Spanky had a great idea. Before the punishment was to be delivered, he put a book down the back of his pants to cushion the blow. Spanky's father, as he put his son over his knee said, "Son, this is going to hurt me a lot more than it is going to hurt you." Spanky mumbles something like "You can say that again, Pops." As his father lays his hand on his bottom, he gets a big surprise.

I am not sure if that memory has stuck in my mind because growing up, I thought putting a book down my pants might be a good idea if I was ever swatted, or because of what his father said. Today, it is the latter of course. There are going to be times that moving someone off your team might hurt you more or the same that it hurts the person you are moving off. No one ever said leadership is easy. In fact, if it doesn't bother you in some way because of how that person feels (not because you are afraid of how they might feel about you), then you don't care about that person enough and you aren't in the act of nurturing; most likely, you are just negatively performance managing.

The hardest of the hardest things for leaders to do is to move someone off. However, Care to Lead Leaders do it because it is the right thing for that person, for you, and for the entire team and organization. Sometimes it is the only option you have.

I was speaking at a large law firm several months ago and shared the principle of nurturing with their leadership team. The founder of this firm came up to me later and shared how one deceiving star (super chicken) in their organization had affected their entire culture and the tough choice he had to make in moving her off.

He said that for a long time, leaders had regularly been heaping praise, recognition, and awards on mainly one top producer. The hope was that it would continue to "pump her up" and inspire others in the organization. However, unbeknownst to him she was anything but an inspiration to their firm. Even though she was the top producer, she had become a problem for a lot of reasons. Many had come to resent her. Her influence and negativity were quickly spreading throughout the organization

People in the firm started seeing meetings as a regular coronation. This resented deceiving star was continuingly being put on a pedestal. People not only had little respect for her but oftentimes felt defeated because they stopped believing they were capable of achieving the things that this top producer whom they had little respect for had achieved. Some had even given up entirely on reaching their goals.

This leader went on to tell me that the hardest thing to do is to fire someone, but as he had learned of this situation, he felt he had no choice. This super chicken was literally suppressing the productivity of the rest. He said, "The cost of not doing anything and having this negative cancer continue to spread was simply too high." So, he made the difficult decision and let her go. Afterward a somewhat surprisingly thing happened. Not only did people seem to be happier, but the firm had seen a big surge in productivity. People started performing at a much higher level. He said, "Ironically, we did much better without our top producer than we had with her."

There are going to be times when the right thing to do is the hardest thing to do, but the best thing to do for everyone.

Pause, Reflect, and Apply

- Are you having the difficult conversations and making the difficult decisions when needed in moving people up, over, or off? Or are you avoiding and ignoring? What is going to change?

_____

_____

_____

Care More about Those You Lead than What You Fear

In surveys of executives in Europe and America, 85% of them said they had issues or concerns at work they were afraid to address.[3] That is a big number of issues not being raised! Why do we fear having difficult conversations, giving potentially hard-to-accept feedback or just simply being more bold, direct, and honest? I think many leaders deep down know they should, but just can't. There is a good chance (85% chance to be exact) that you probably know a leader or two like this. Maybe you are one yourself? But not all is lost; 85% of us can become more courageous. It all comes back to caring about those you lead.

As a parent many years ago I learned a few things, one specifically about courage, that forever changed how I looked at leadership. At the time we had five children living in a fairly small home. Our second youngest child, Kelli, who was four, had come into our room where my wife and I were reading—she was in a bit of a panic. Our youngest, Jeff, who was two at the time, had fallen asleep on the couch and it had gotten dark. She was very worried because both she and Jeff were very afraid of the dark.

We assured her it was okay, there was nothing to be afraid of and that Jeff was fine. Because of her sweet nature (which is still just as sweet today), she didn't say a thing and quietly left our room. After a minute or two, my wife decided to go check on both our young daughter and little son. As she turned the corner into the living room, she saw something that she would never forget. There lying on the couch next to each other were Kelli and Jeff. When she got closer, she could see that Kelli was laying over her baby brother protecting him from the thing they both really feared.

I learned two important lessons that day. First, to never dismiss someone's fears or concerns. Their fears and concerns are as real as your own personal fears and concerns, regardless of how young or inexperienced they may be. This was a great lesson in empathy to me. The second lesson I learned, and the most relevant to what we are talking about, is that courage doesn't mean you aren't afraid; it is a matter of caring more about something than what you are afraid of. Kelli cared about her little brother so much that she was willing to overcome her greatest fear (the dark) to protect him. You too can overcome your fears and have greater courage when you care more about something than the thing you fear.

A great deal of what you do as a nourishing leader requires courage. Moving people up, over, and off can be hard because it requires having difficult but critical conversations in which you might have to provide bold, direct, and honest feedback. Sometimes you are going to have to make decisions that could negatively affect how others feel about you. The fear of being wrong, the fear of being criticized, the fear of not being liked, the fear of failure, and the fear of what others might think about you weigh on leaders every day. Leadership can be lonely. But Care to Lead Leaders have a bigger picture for their teams and organizations. Leaders who deeply care focus not on what's best for them personally, but instead what's best for the people they lead. They are more connected and concerned with those they lead than what they fear. As a result, the difficult discussions become less difficult, hard decisions become a little easier, the fear of being wrong, the fear of being criticized, and the fear of what others might think about you are replaced with the fear of people failing to reach their full potential. Although nurturing might be difficult at times, leaders exchange being uncomfortable in the short term for inspiring successes in the long term.

When you care enough to do the difficult things as a leader, your team and others take notice. Nurturing builds trust and connection with those you lead. People are more likely to board the rocket, as we talked about in the introduction, because they have bought into you and where you want them to go.

Roll Up Your Sleeves

Nurturing is a proactive process that takes time, lots of effort, and sometimes even tears. But leadership was never about sitting around doing little and hoping for big and inspiring results, right? In addition to working the nurturing grid we talked about previously, here are four more things to help you and those you lead.

Acknowledge and Know Your People

A number of years ago I was asked to serve as the head of a church congregation of about 800 people and families. Clergy are not paid in my religion, so it was all volunteer (about 25 or more hours a week in addition to my full-time job). I willingly accepted the assignment/calling because I felt it was the right thing to do, though I knew it would be a great challenge.

This leadership assignment/calling would require that I minister to this congregation, listen intently and counsel them on their struggles, grieve with them through tragedy, and teach whenever I could. After my first Sunday as the new leader I came home exhausted, but fulfilled. I felt I had done a pretty good job given it was my first day. I asked my wife, Terri, how she thought I had done. Of course, she had lots of positive things to say, but she did point out one thing I could do differently as well.

She said, "Mike, you may not have even realized you did this, but I was watching you in the hall after church and noticed you didn't act any differently." I said, "That's good, because I shouldn't really act any differently, I am the same person I was before I was called to this position."

She said, "True, but in your new leadership position people expect you to acknowledge them. You went down the hall and barely made eye contact with anyone. I saw a number of people wanting you to acknowledge them, but you must have had so much on your mind."

I said, "I did have a lot on my mind, and I was heading to a meeting I was already running late for." Her response was gentle and simple, "Honey, it is important to acknowledge people in this leadership position regardless of how 'busy' you might be. They want you to look into their eyes and acknowledge them by their name."

She recounted how it made her feel when church leaders had acknowledged and remembered her name. She was right, and I made it a point from that day forward to smile more and acknowledge people by their name, regardless of how much I had on my mind or how busy I was.

How important is it for leaders to acknowledge people? Very important! In my career, the leaders that took the time to reach out and acknowledge me at a gathering or meeting, though they may have been my bosses' boss, have had an important and positive impact on me. I felt valued.

Nurturing is also about knowing people personally so that you can understand them with certainty. How well do you know those you lead? Do you know their desires, aspirations, and challenges? Do you know the things that worry them or the things that they fear? Do you talk about their families, hobbies, and successes? Only through knowing your people can you understand your people and what they need so that you can help them grow.

In speaking to a graduating class of cadets at the Royal British Military Academy in 1944 Dwight D. Eisenhower said the following to the soon-to-be officers:

> You must know every single one of your men. It is not enough that you are the best soldier in that unit, that you are the strongest, the toughest, the most durable, the best equipped, technically—you must be their leader, their father, their mentor, even if you're half their age. You must understand their problems. You must keep them out of trouble; if they get in trouble, you must be the one who goes to their rescue. That cultivation of human understanding between you and your men is the one part that you must yet master, and you must master it quickly."[4]

Pause, Reflect, and Apply

- How well do you know those you lead? What can you do to know and understand them better?

  _____

  _____

  _____

Spend Time with Them

You can't nourish your people if you don't know your people. You can't know your people unless you are spending time with your people. You can't build relationships and trust with your people unless you are nurturing them, spending time with them, and getting to know each of them.

Leadership is a relationship job and many times an extrovert activity. Even if you are an introvert by nature, you are going to have to put your extrovert hat on from time to time to do leadership right and build important relationships with those you lead. Closing your door won't work. Saying you are too busy won't work. Thinking that employee nurturing can wait won't work. Being out and public does work.

Spending time with those you lead is critical to building understanding, trust, and connection. The only way you can strengthen relationships is to invest in those relationships, which requires you to be present. The only way you can get valuable feedback and help and support those you lead is to get out from behind the desk.

I knew of a CEO who was leading a 50,000-person organization. He could have made excuses and said he was too busy and there were too many employees to connect with and many would have believed he was right. But because making a connection from the top was important to him, he came up with a way to make it happen. While he was traveling, he would always ensure the meetings he held were in company offices. He would schedule time out of his day to walk the floors of the office greeting people, asking them about their families, hobbies, work challenges, and things they were proud of—general chitchat. Weeks or months later when he would return to that same office, he would review his notes from the previous visit and then greet everyone he could by name and ask for updates on each of them and their families. Did it make an impact? Yes, it made an impact on those employees whom he spoke with and it made an impact on the entire company as word spread about his thoughtfulness. It also made an impact on him as he felt more connected to the people doing the "real work." Additionally, he was able to gauge morale, gather ideas, and receive input and feedback on how to improve. Of course, this CEO wasn't able to get to every employee, but he made a genuine effort to get to as many as he could.

Entrepreneur Richard Branson once said, "The best ideas come from people who get out from behind their desks and chat directly with others, learn from them and build trust." He practices what he preaches. A while back, a friend of mine shared the following personal story of Branson with me:

Some years ago, I was given the task of organizing a medical symposium in the south of England. One of the hotels I visited while checking suitable venues was flying the Virgin flag (Richard Branson's company). So, when I arrived at the front desk, I asked Mary, the receptionist, if she'd ever met Richard Branson.

Her response absolutely blew me away. She said, "Yes, and he's the most wonderful man I've ever met in my life."

She went on to relate that shortly after buying the hotel, Mr. Branson made an appointment to see the hotel manager. On arrival the first person he met was Mary, who happened to be cleaning the carpet at the time. She knew who he was of course and said, "You'll be wanting to see the manager." He replied, "Yes, but tell me about yourself first." He spent 20 minutes with Mary before keeping his appointment with the manager.

He spent all day at the hotel, spending at least 20 minutes with each member of the staff from the top to the person who cleaned the toilets. BUT, that wasn't the punchline.

Six months later, Branson paid another visit. Mary had been promoted to receptionist, but he recognized her immediately and addressed her by name. "Not only that," she said, "he remembered that I had a little girl and what her name was, and that she was about to have her tonsils removed, and he wanted to know if she was all right. He was like that with every member of the staff."

My friend went on to say,

Now, I don't believe that Richard Branson has that good a memory. He must have written a lot of notes after his first visit, and he must have spent a lot of time reading them over again before that second visit. That must have been time-consuming, but it shows the importance he places on human relationships and that he devotes the same importance to the relationship irrespective of the person's rank. Everyone I've met who knows Richard Branson personally has told me the same thing ... that he's the most wonderful person in the world to work for.

If the aforementioned CEO and Richard Branson could make the time to visit employees on such a personal level, what's a leader's excuse with organizations and teams far less than the thousands these leaders lead?

Spending time with those you lead is a nurturing activity, but it also creates greater trust and safe climates of openness—which we talked about in chapter 2.

- Are you spending enough time with those you lead? Do you feel you are connecting enough with your people? What will you do differently?

_____

_____

_____

Listen to Your People

I can remember about 10 years or so ago sitting in the office of a colleague and friend of mine opening up about some recent challenges I was having and being somewhat vulnerable. In a matter of minutes this person had pulled out his phone and was going through email. I didn't know I could be so boring, but I also didn't realize he could be so insensitive. I immediately changed the topic and then kindly excused myself. That was the last time I would ever have a conversation like that with him again. My trust of this person plummeted. If you choose to listen to those you lead in a similar manner, it will be the last time people open up to you as well.

Nurturing requires active listening. You can't care about and develop people if you don't listen to what they are saying. And people won't openly share with you if they don't trust that you care. My wife has a lot of friends who consider her a very good friend, if not a best friend. It has always amazed me how easily she attracts people to her. I have found the reason is due to her ability to truly listen to others and take a genuine interest in their lives.

Many of us, however, love to talk way too much about ourselves and attempt to solve other's problems while failing to truly listen to what is being said. We really like being interesting to others instead of taking an interest in them. And if something isn't interesting to us and we don't have anything interesting to say about ourselves, we stop listening all together. If this doesn't describe you, there is a high probability that you know someone whom it does describe.

With more and more virtual interactions occurring in business than ever before, listening is becoming even harder. I would bet that most leaders are doing their fair share of multitasking on conference calls these days, including one-on-one calls with those they lead. How do I know this? Because I have been the recipient of such calls in my not-too-distant past. If you closely pay attention you will know as well. The awkward silence that makes you feel you are the only one present. The long uncomfortable pause before responding to your question, followed up by asking you to repeat it. The keyboard periodically hammering in the background. The loud restful breathing and sometimes even snoring. Yep, we know when someone isn't paying attention, don't we? Those you lead know as well.

Even in person we can feel like someone isn't present. His eyes might be focused on you, but it feels like his mind is focused somewhere else. Many of the same signs we receive on calls also happen face-to-face.

Leaders who actually listen not only convey warmth and trust but also considerably stand out from those who don't.

Which kind of leader do you want to be? You can't tell people to board a rocket if you never listened long enough to understand their concerns, challenges, hopes, and dreams.

Here are five actions you can start doing today to become better at listening to those you lead.

Listen First, Fix Second   I remember seeing a picture once of a huge orange fish with its mouth wide open going after a big piece of bait on a fisherman's hook. The caption read, "Sometimes it pays to keep your mouth shut." Many times, leaders should choose to do the same. Listening is about trying to understand before trying to help. Leaders by virtue of what they do fix things, so it's not uncommon to jump in and a find solution before understanding if that is what the person they are talking to even needs. Oftentimes what is needed is just for someone to quietly and attentively listen.

Focus on What's Being Said   A big problem with communication in general is that too many people, including many leaders, focus on what they are going to say next and miss what the other person is actually saying. For example, they try to be understood without trying to understand, leading to interrupting and tuning out what the other person is actually saying. In your next communication, force yourself to really listen to what is being said, instead of what you need to say. You will be surprised how much better the conversation goes.

Body Language Matters   Many years ago, I was in a job interview and one particular person on the panel just stared at me the entire time with an expressionless face and in a slouched position with her arms folded. I thought through the whole interview that she didn't really like me all that much and this wasn't going so well. I ended up getting the job, and it turned out that she actually did like me! Her body language that day was not indicative of how she felt; it was just how she presented herself in meetings. Boy, did I read her wrong!

Your body language sends a strong message of how well you are listening and how much you are interested. People are only going to share and open up to the level they are comfortable doing so. An awareness of your body language is critical so that you are sending the right message.

Here are some tips to ensure that those you are talking with know that you are listening and that you care:

- **Open yourself.** Avoid folding your arms, crossing your legs (if sitting), or hiding your hands. Instead, uncross your legs and put your feet flat on the floor, open your arms, and use gestures where your palms can be seen. Not only does this convey you are listening to the person you are talking to but also signals to your brain that you are listening as well

- **Lean in.** Leaning in conveys a strong message that you are interested in what the other person is saying. There is research that shows that leaning in creates greater verbal output in those being listened to.

- **Tilt head slightly in one direction.** Tilting your head is the universal sign that you are giving the person you are talking to your ear.

- **Have good eye contact.** This one seems obvious, but unfortunately it isn't to some. If you fail to make eye contact, or even worse become easily distracted with things around you, the message becomes clear to the person that you are talking to that you just don't care.

- **Nod when the person is talking.** A nod every 10 seconds or so conveys that you hear what is being said.

- **Smile occasionally.** Smiling brings a warmth to your listening.

One solid way to find out the types of signals you are sending is to simply ask others what they think those signals are.

Restate When the person you are listening to is done talking, check for understanding. Restate what has been said. If you know you will have to restate what is being shared, you will stay more focused on listening to what is being said.

Clarify Closely related to restating is asking clarifying questions. "So how did it make you feel?" and "Is this what you are meaning by this?" are examples of clarifying questions. It ensures that you are really *understanding* what is being said, not just hearing what is said. Clarifying questions help you get to the heart of what people are saying and how they feel, which is at the heart of what Care to Lead Leaders do.

Very few things say trust and connection like active listening does. There are lots of opportunities for you to practice 😊.

Help Them, Delegate to Them, and Empower Them

Nurturing Care to Lead Leaders empower others. Empowering and delegating provides those you lead opportunities to expand, grow, and contribute in unique ways.

Fresh out of graduate school I considered myself the best at doing what I was trained at doing. I was an instructional technologist, and I was pretty good at it, and the numerous kudos and recognition I received only validated it.

However, I was soon promoted into a supervisor role and couldn't do everything that I had done before. I had to let go of some things. That was tough, and I fought it—I still wanted to make every decision and receive all of the praise that goes with doing amazing work. Selfish, I know, but I was young. Instead of delegating to and empowering others to make decisions and do the work, I worked hours and hours doing my day job as a supervisor and pounding out training design and development far after everyone had gone home.

I couldn't sustain that pace for much longer and went to my leader at the time with the problem. She asked me a number of questions about what my day looked like and then said this: "Mike, your problem is that you think you are the only one who can do what you do." I looked a little puzzled. She said, "If you are going to lead and get done everything you want done and more, you better learn how to let go and give others a chance to prove their worth. There are people on your team that can do what you do; you just need to help them, delegate to them, and empower them to get there."

Wow! That was a light bulb moment and rescued me from the piles of stress that I had heaped on myself due to my rookie mistake of not letting go. I eventually realized that by helping, delegating, and empowering others to do the types of things that I was doing that I would indeed have more time, less stress, greater retention rates, and honestly there would be more creativity, and, in many cases, even better design and development. My team would be better balanced, feel more valued, and have more development opportunities as a result. It was truly a win-win! And that's what happened.

But helping, delegating, and empowering others is difficult because of trust. How can I trust those I delegate to or empower? And how can they trust me and feel empowered? There are four things you must do to generate the type of trust necessary for empowerment to work: provide proper training and tools; be clear on what empowerment means and what it doesn't mean; help them feel safe; and provide support, encouragement, and praise.

Provide Proper Training and Tools This is probably one of the main reasons leaders don't delegate; they don't want to take the time to train. But in the long run it will save you by investing in the short run.

There was a joke I once heard that illustrates this really well.

A brand-new hotel employee was asked to clean the elevators and report back to his supervisor once the task had been completed. The end of the day came and the employee never reported back. His boss simply assumed that like the rest of those he had hired that the employee had quit.

However, after three days the supervisor bumped into the new employee. He was inside one of the elevators cleaning it. The boss, in an accusatory voice, asked, "You surely haven't been cleaning these elevators for three days, have you?"

"Yes, sir, I have," said the employee. "This is a huge job, and I'm not done yet. Do you realize there are over fifty-five of them, two on each floor, and sometimes they are not even there!"

Think about it ...

Though this example is more about day-to-day job duties than it is about delegating and empowering, it makes an important point. You must provide to those you delegate to proper instructions, tools, and contacts to correctly do what is being asked. To throw those you lead out of the nest and ask them to fly is setting them up for failure in a big way. People won't feel completely empowered if they are regularly failing at the things you delegate to them.

Be Clear on What Empowerment Means and What It Doesn't Mean Those you empower need to clearly understand expectations. How will they know when they are being successful? What type of quality work are you looking for? If they run into obstacles, where do they go?

Lack of communication is often cited as one of the main reasons leaders fail. Super clear communication as it pertains to empowering is critical.

Help Them Feel Safe We have already talked about this at length in chapter 2. When people are given the green light of empowerment, they must feel safe from the beginning. If they don't, those you lead won't be willing to take risks. Empowerment doesn't happen unless you have created a climate of safety.

Provide Support, Encouragement, and Praise In order to be successful with helping others feel empowered and continue to feel empowered, you must meet with them regularly. Have them return and report on how they are doing with things they were delegated. Provide your positive support and encouragement. Praise them when they do well. Create a habit of giving regular feedback on what you are seeing and ask them for feedback on what they are seeing. And coach as needed.

You Can't Nurture if You Don't Make an Effort to Understand

A 10-year-old boy walked up to the counter of a soda shop and climbed onto a stool. He caught the eye of the waitress and asked, "How much is an ice cream sundae?"

"Fifty cents," the waitress replied. The boy reached into his pockets, pulled out a handful of change, and began counting. The waitress frowned impatiently. After all, she had other customers to wait on.

The boy squinted up at the waitress. "How much is a dish of plain ice cream?" he asked. The waitress sighed and rolled her eyes. "Thirty-five cents," she said with a note of irritation.

Again, the boy counted his coins. At last, he said, "I'll have the plain ice cream, please." He put a quarter and two nickels on the counter. The waitress took the coins, brought the ice cream, and walked away.

About ten minutes later, she returned and found the ice cream dish empty. The boy was gone. She picked up the empty dish—then swallowed hard.

There on the counter, next to the wet spot where the dish had been, were two nickels and five pennies. The boy had had enough for a sundae, but he had ordered plain ice cream so he could have enough to leave her a tip.

Unfortunately, it is all too common to tell ourselves stories about others without taking the time to really understand. Separating truth and what we are thinking from our emotions, including those of worry, disappointment, hurt feelings, irritation, and anger, is hard. Someone once said, "The greatest mistake we humans make in our relationships is that we listen half, understand quarter, think zero, and react double." There can be no nurturing without an effort of understanding. And there are moments you are going to need to remove yourself completely, for a period of time, from the situation.

24-Hour Rule

Several years ago, I was sitting in a parent meeting for the upcoming high school basketball season. The head coach talked about policies, travel, schedules, and so forth and then the athletic director spoke. He pleaded with parents to follow what he called the *24-hour rule*.

"Whenever you have a gripe with a coach about lack of playing time, the position your son is playing, or anything else, don't approach him right after the game," he said. "If you do, the coach may act in a way he shouldn't, which may cause you to act in a way you shouldn't."

He suggested instead that parents wait 24 hours. This gives them the chance to sleep on the problem, clearly think about the problem, and then deal with it in a more level-headed way if necessary. This suggested rule gives you time to separate your emotion from the situation so you can instead come from a heartfelt desire to understand, not immediately condemn.

The 24-hour rule can work in many situations, such as waiting to send off an email that you will later regret, taking a time-out in the middle of a meeting to collect yourself before you blow up, or waiting before you talk to an employee who made a huge frustrating mistake. It might only take you an hour or less to think things through, not 24 hours, but it just needs to be long enough to try to understand and cool off and not say or do something you regret.

Empathy

Empathy is a tool to understanding. It is feeling what it's like to be another person. Although you can't literally be another person, you can get close to hearing what she hears, seeing what she sees, and feeling what she feels. It requires you to walk in someone else's shoes, to put on their hat and try to vicariously experience all that they are experiencing so that you can understand them better. The more we demonstrate empathy, the better we can understand why someone feels the way he does. If we fail to have empathy, then we ultimately fail those we lead.

You aren't a weak leader when you demonstrate empathy, as some have believed, but instead a strong Care to Lead Leader who understands the effect that decisions have on others. Empathy helps heart-based leaders to manage difficult situations in ways that ultimately create better feelings and outcomes for everyone because of a heightened understanding. It is also a critical skill in helping Care to Lead Leaders effectively nurture. You can't appropriately move someone up, over, or off if you don't really understand the impact each choice has.

Next time you are struggling with a decision, a response to a negative situation or a reaction to something you did or said; take a time-out and put on the hat and shoes of those who your decision or reaction affects or affected.

Pause, Reflect, and Apply

- Do you regularly make an effort to practice empathy in your leadership? What kind of difference would empathy make in your leadership? How can you start demonstrating more empathy in your role as a leader?

  _____

  _____

  _____

The Fundamental Attribution Error

A big barrier to understanding others is our practice of something we all do. One morning, I was taking my kids to school. As I was driving down the long road from the hill on which we live, someone was tailgating behind me. I am not fond of people who tailgate, so I began to create a lot of stories in my head about why the inconsiderate person behind me was following so closely. I thought to myself, "What's your problem?" and "You aren't going to get there any quicker by riding my bumper; how inconsiderate can you be!" In short, I was completely jumping to conclusions.

Now, of course, when I tailgate someone down this same hill it's because I am in a hurry! I am frustrated because they are going too slow and I say things to myself, "What's your problem?" and "I have somewhere to get quickly, put a quarter in it, and make it go!" Do you see what's happening here? When someone tailgates me, it's because they are rude and inconsiderate. But when I do the same thing it's because I have somewhere I need to get to fast.

What I have described is called the *fundamental attribution error*. It is human nature, and we do it all the time. It's the same reason that when you see parents angrily scolding their children in a restaurant you think, "Get a grip; you have some real anger issues." Then you go home and scold your children and think, "My children are so misbehaved!"

The fundamental attribution error is simply relating behavior we don't like to someone's character and ignoring situational factors when judging that person. It's believing that people do bad things because they are bad people. Of course, when we do the same thing it's not because we are bad; it's simply justified. Most of us want to give people the benefit of the doubt, but with limited information, we fill in our own perceptions, biases, and information—we again create stories. We jump to conclusions. Have you ever done something that you don't believe represents your true character? Of course you have, and so have others.

It is common for leaders to also get caught up in the fundamental attribution error. For example, let's say someone you lead by the name of Jane fails to meet an important deadline on an assignment you gave her. Your immediate thought might be, "I made sure that Jane understood when this was due; she just didn't care that much." That statement inside of your mind at that moment is developing into a label of Jane and making you angrier and angrier as you think about it, even though you missed a similar deadline to your boss three months ago and for good reason. In this instance, you failed to consider anything outside of Jane's "bad" behavior. Instead you chose to shoot off a short and direct email in a tone that she would clearly understand to let her know that her lateness was unacceptable and that you need her to have it done tomorrow, no exceptions. However, if you had taken the time to really understand why Jane missed the deadline you might have found out that your instructions were not as clear as you thought, or that she just didn't have the resources to get it done, or that Jane may have not been the right person for this assignment in the first place. Now, the blame should be on you instead, not Jane. But you failed to try to understand.

When leaders are caught in a fundamental attribution error, they might write people off and create biases that make it difficult, if not impossible, to effectively nurture. Nurturing is as much about understanding as it is about developing. You might not relate to the previous scenario, but I believe with 100% certainty that if you looked hard enough, you can find situations in your leadership where this error is a problem.

The fundamental attribution error often leads to poor decision-making, a myopic view of things, mistrust of others, and a big risk of losing your falling stars and steady stars who with the right nurturing could have become rock stars. What can you do?

First of all, you have to be aware. I challenge you to start thinking about the error and catching yourself in it and seeing when others are doing it. Second, stop yourself and ask yourself and others questions instead. Don't let your nearsighted emotions get the better of you. Once you have thought through why it might have happened, talk to that employee and others to find out what really happened. Third, spend time with those you lead. One of the best ways to overcome the fundamental attribution error is to build strong relationships with those you lead. This is one of the reasons that when I work with teams, I encourage them to spend lots of time together on a more personal level. Trust and understanding improves as our relationships improve.

Pause, Reflect, and Apply

- In the next couple of days, focus on looking for the fundamental attribution error anywhere you can find it: at work, home, church, or any number of other places. Next, start looking for it in your leadership and work on overcoming it by asking questions to understand and by building better relationships.

  _____

  _____

  _____

Care to Lead Leader Nurture Takeaways

- Focus on nurturing, not performance managing.

- Every person on your team and in your organizations comes to you with different experiences, histories, gifts and talents, skills and perspectives. Don't cookie-cut your leadership.

- Nurturing is about caring enough to have the courage to actively move people up, over, or off. Doing nothing is never a Care to Lead Leader option.

- The majority of a Care to Lead Leader's time is spent on moving people up.

- Courage doesn't mean you aren't afraid; it means you care more about something than what you fear.

- Nurturing is a proactive process that requires you to roll up your sleeves by regularly acknowledging, getting to know, spending time with, listening to, and helping, delegating, and empowering those you lead.

- It will be difficult to nurture if you don't make the effort to understand.

Notes

1. Gallup, *State of the American Workplace* (Washington, DC: Gallup Inc., 2017), 80, 110.

2. Margaret Heffernan, "Forget the Pecking Order at Work," *Ted: Ideas Worth Spreading,* Video File, May 2015, https://www.ted.com/talks/margaret_heffernan_why_it_s_time_to_forget_the_pecking_order_at_work.

3. Margaret Heffernan, "Dare to Disagree," *Ted: Ideas Worth Spreading,* Video File, June 2012, https://www.ted.com/talks/margaret_heffernan_dare_to_disagree.

4. Keith Grint, *Leadership, Management and Command: Rethinking D-Day* (New York: Palgrave MacMillan, 2008), 187.

Chapter 4

Inspire

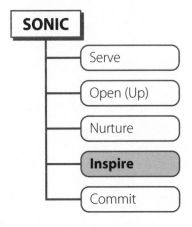

*If you don't know where you are going, why you are
going there, or how you are going to get there, it
doesn't matter much which way you go because
although you may end up somewhere, to your team it
will always feel like nowhere.*

A businessman was once on a long flight when the first warning that something was wrong came over the PA system. The pilot asked everyone to take their seats and fasten their seat belts.

After a while another announcement came over the PA. The pilot calmly told the passengers that they would not be offering beverage service due to unexpected turbulence on its way.

As the businessman looked around the aircraft, he noticed some of the passengers becoming a little worried. Later, the pilot announced that in addition to no beverage service, there would be no meal service due to the expected turbulence.

The plane came on the storm shortly after this last announcement. Thunder could be heard all around the aircraft and lightning could be seen lighting up the dark sky. Within a matter of minutes, the plane was being tossed around like a small toy with passengers becoming more and more fearfully alarmed by every big bump. One moment the plane was lifted and the next it was dropped as if it was crashing.

The businessman was also becoming somewhat anxious, and as he looked around the plane nearly all the passengers were upset and alarmed. Some were praying. The future seemed ominous and many were wondering if they would make it through the storm.

Then suddenly he saw a little girl out of the corner of his eye. Apparently, the storm meant nothing to her. She had tucked her feet beneath her as she sat on her seat. She was reading a book and everything within her small world was calm and orderly. Sometimes she closed her eyes, then she would read again; then she would straighten her legs, but worry and fear seemed to not be on her mind. When the plane was being buffeted by the terrible storm, when it quickly and aggressively jolted this way and that, as it rose and fell with frightening harshness, when all the adults were scared half to death, the little girl was completely composed and unafraid. The businessman was completely amazed!

When the plane landed passengers hurried to get their stuff and get off. However, this little girl sat and calmly waited for everyone to exit the plane. The businessman decided to wait as well so he could talk to this little girl.

After having commented about the storm and the behavior of the plane, he asked why she hadn't been afraid.

The little girl replied, "Sir, my dad is the pilot, and he is taking me home."

When you have invested time in serving, opening up, and nurturing, your people believe in you as well. They know that you care and have their best interest at heart. They feel safe in going where you are taking them, regardless of the adversity encountered and how difficult the journey might get. Now it's time to super inspire and continue to inspire them to go to places they have never been before and to do things they have never done before. It's time to put the foot on the pedal and accelerate what your team is capable of doing. You have done the hard work to this point of mixing and getting the first three ingredients right through building trust (serve), connection (open up), and capabilities (nurture). Now it's time to start getting your team(s) and organization(s) excited, focused, and moving toward greatness by adding the fourth ingredient of the formula—inspire.

To start, every person you lead is going to need to know where you want them to go, why you are going there, and how they will get there.

The Where, Why, and How

The where, why, and how are three questions every Care to Lead Leader uses to help inspire their team to great results. These three questions are about inspiring your people to board rockets and getting them to stick with, stay loyal to, and focused on what you are trying to achieve (the end result).

The Where: The Vision

I have always loved the following adapted quote from Lewis Carroll's classic *Alice in Wonderland*.

Cat: Where are you going?

Alice: Which way should I go?

Cat: That depends on where you are going.

Alice: I don't know.

Cat: Then it doesn't matter which way you go.[1]

Do you know where you are going? Where are you taking those you lead? Do they know where you are taking them? Because if you don't know where you are going, it doesn't matter much which way you go because although you may end up somewhere, to your team it will always feel like nowhere. If you don't clearly spell out the where, eventually your team just won't care.

Imagine yourself out in a row boat in the middle of a lake and in a dense heavy fog. You and your team are told by the leader of the row boat to keep rowing, keep rowing, keep rowing; but never once did she tell you where you were going. How long are you going to keep rowing if you don't know where you are going?

You and your crewmates will tire out and burn out eventually as you row to nowhere. Being told to row without any hint of land results in people who are less inspired and less motivated to keep going. Your crewmates are going to start complaining, trust is going to wane, and everyone's drive to do this together (the rowing) is going to quickly deteriorate. Some might continue to still row, others won't, ensuring that you row in circles over and over again. Eventually everyone stops rowing altogether.

Now imagine a boat in which not only does the leader clearly tell you and the team where you are going but also why you are going there. You not only have a picture of where you are going but a purpose as well.

Which boat would you want to be in? Which boat do you want to be a leader in?

The Team Vision With most teams I have worked with over the years, there is usually some alignment to the bigger organization's overall vision (if they have one), which is really important. But what almost all teams (small and large) lack is their own vision. Although the overall organization's vision has the power to unite that organization as a whole to row together to the same big island, a team vision speaks specifically to your team or team's role in helping the organization get there. That vision is the unique position in the larger organization that your team or teams intend to fill. It's their own inspiring dream of becoming bigger and more successful so that they can help the organization as a whole become bigger and more successful.

Care to Lead Leaders recognize the important value of a team vision because it inspires people to do great things. The purpose of the vision is to take people and teams to places they have never been. It's the difference we talked about way back in the introduction of getting people to take rocket rides versus predictable and uninspiring subway rides. When a vision includes a clear way to get there and the why behind getting there (more on that later), it becomes a fundamental tool for Care to Lead Leaders to inspire people and teams to take action and become greater than they ever believed they could.

A great vision is a dream that leaders are excited about, talk about, and deeply care about. It becomes a dream that others want to not only follow but share as well.

Visions move teams and organizations through difficult things. When obstacles are presented and seemingly impossible circumstances arise, leaders are able to move their teams and organizations through rough waters because everyone on the team is committed to realizing the dream together.

What is important to a vision is that people feel connected to it. When they are connected to it, they understand it, are aligned to it, are deeply inspired by it, and are eager to share it. People want to feel connected to something bigger than themselves. Studies show that only 44% of employees believe they even see a connection. Connecting your people's goals to the overall goals of the organization dramatically increases engagement. When there is a clear alignment, employees are 3.5 times more likely to be engaged.[2] Having a connected vision is huge!

Including your team in the writing of the vision is the perfect way to begin to inspire them around that vision. People are more likely to buy in and support what they help create. Here are some questions that you can ask as you meet together to formulate your own vision. Spend time discussing and diving into each one.

- Why does our team need a vision?
- What problems are we trying to solve? What difference would solving these problems have on our team and to people inside and outside of our team and organization?
- What does success look like on our team?
- What is our dream for our team? How do our larger organization's values align to this dream? How does the bigger organization's vision align to our dreams?
- If our dream for our team were to come true, what would look different on our team and across our organization? When we have realized our dream what will people remember about us long after we are gone?

Asking and discussing each of these questions will help your team(s) to start formulating their vision.

Note: If you are a CEO or president of a company and don't currently have a vision, these questions can help in guiding you to create one.

Here are some thoughts to keep in mind as you are fleshing out your vision:

- **Keep it aligned.** Your team(s) should completely understand the organization or company vision. What does success look like for the larger organization or company? The team vision should perfectly support and align with that overall vision.

- **Keep it value based.** Your vision should be in complete alignment with the values of your organization.

- **Keep it short.** Vision statements are best when kept to one sentence, two at a maximum. It needs to be something people can commit to memory so that it is easily shared. It should be something that looks clear and big on a poster, for example.

- **Keep it simple.** Don't include technical jargon, business buzzwords, or fluffy language. People inside and outside your organization should quickly understand what it means.

- **Keep it real.** A vision needs to be ambitious, but not so ambitious that it's impossible.

- **Keep it measurable.** When you are having success, what does that look like? If your team vision, for example, is, "Our team sets the standard for customer service in the company," how will you know you are arriving or have arrived? That's a discussion you would have with your team.

Why Visions Don't Stick If a vision fails to be adopted by a team, the ownership of that failure rests squarely on the shoulders of the leader. The reason visions don't stick is simple: leaders aren't giving the attention it needs because they don't care enough about it. Once you understand the power of the vision to inspire your people, you won't stop thinking and talking about it.

Have you ever learned something or done something that you couldn't wait to share with others? We tend to talk about and share those things that excite us the most. If you are excited about your team vision, your team will be excited about it and naturally share it. You will plaster it all over the office, talk about it at every meeting and employee one-on-ones, and even share it with those outside of your team. If you aren't excited about it, you won't. If that's the case, you need to ask yourself whether it's even the right vision.

Visions don't stick simply because they are either not exciting enough or fail to be at the top of the mind of those who are supposed to be living it. Make it stick!

Pause, Reflect, and Apply

- Does your team have a vision? If you do, how excited are you and your team about it? Is there anything you need to change? If you don't have a team vision, set a date with your team to create one using the provided guidelines above.

The Why: The Purpose

Now that you know where you are going, it is just as important to instill why you are going there. Although a vision (the what) can inspire people, it won't last long unless you have a purpose (the why) for getting there.

I once heard former Ritz Carlton president Horst Schulze say that when he hired hotel managers, he would ask them what their vision was for the hotel. If they didn't have a vision, he wouldn't hire them because they were managers who simply wanted to just take care of the hotel and maintain what already existed, not really lead it. He said, leaders have a vision and ask, "How do I make it better, how do I align my employees to it, how do I make sure it is good for my employees, how do I make sure they join me?" However, Schulze said, leaders don't just tell people to do this and do that. They say, here is why we are doing this.

Those on your team and in your organization have to have a compelling reason for doing what they are doing. A purpose inspires lasting behavioral change; it is the reason your people get excited to get up in the morning and do what they do throughout the day. When people are less engaged it's usually not because of what they are doing, it's because they forgot the why behind what they are doing.

People seek meaning and significance in what they do. Research cited in the *Harvard Business Review* revealed that "when workers were asked how important it was that their lives be meaningful, 83 percent said 'very important' and another 15 percent said 'fairly important.'"[3] That's a total of 98% of people who feel meaning matters. And a number

Do You Care to Lead?

of studies have confirmed that employees are likely to stay longer in jobs, give up a big chunk of their salary, put in more time at work, and take less time off for a job that offers them meaning.

During my corporate career most of my work was in the learning, performance, and quality space. In the training materials that we created, it was always important to start with a well-thought-out WIIFM, which means, "What's in it for me?" I came to find that if you could help learners understand what's in it for them (the why), it wouldn't matter how you delivered the training; they would find a way to learn it. People become motivated to learn when they are clear on the why, or the purpose for learning it, and what it means to them.

Likewise, members of your team(s) and organization are also more motivated if they know the purpose behind why they are doing what they are doing. If you want those you lead to not only board a rocket but also loyally take the journey with you, they have to understand the purpose behind why you are taking them there. It's the glue that holds everything together and commits people to the where. And your purpose needs to be clearly aligned from the individual to the larger organization. Every person you lead needs to know their why and how it aligns to the bigger why, just as your vision should align to the bigger vision (the where).

A team might have the vision to be the standard for customer service in the company, but why is that even important? Why does it matter to each member on the team? Why does it matter to the larger organization that they become the standard?

Here are some questions you can discuss to help your team define and get to their why, their purpose. Let's use the simple example of a corporate security team that has responsibilities of protecting company buildings across the country to demonstrate how this works.

1. What do each of us personally bring in terms of skills, gifts, and talents to the team? What do we bring to the organization that is uniquely ours together? These questions help you begin to formulate the why. *As a security team, we have a unique set of talents and skills to protect property and people.*

2. Why does anyone care about what we do? *People care about going home peacefully and safely every night. People want to know that their property when left at work is secure.* With this question you are starting to get to the pain people feel when you don't do your job well.

3. What gets us excited about coming to work every day? Spend some time on this question. It is going to be the thing that inspires people in what they are doing. *We are excited because we are helping people have peace of mind.*

4. Why do we do what we do? This question is at the heart of what you are trying to define and becomes the final question in helping you formulate your purpose. *We do what we do to keep employees safe so that they can go home to their families each night and make sure they aren't wondering if their property is being taken care of.*

Pause, Reflect, and Apply

- Does your team have a purpose? If you do, does it inspire them? Is there anything you need to change? If you don't have a purpose, set a date with your team to create one by using the provided questions above to help guide you.

  _____

  _____

  _____

Regularly reminding those you lead why they do what they do is a sure way to get them to where you are trying to go. Let's now move on to the how.

The How: The Goal(s)

Now that you have the where and the why, we move on to the how. You can have a great vision (the where) and you can even know the purpose (the why), but because you are challenging your team to do bigger and better things than they have ever done before, you must address the how. The how is about helping those you lead get to and realize the where (the vision). A team strategic plan and individual goals is the recipe (the how) for getting there.

The Team Strategic Plan When I work with teams, I always ask them to share with me their plan for the year that aligns with the bigger organization's focus. If they have one, it is often a 5- to 10+-page strategic plan containing 15 to 30 goals and hundreds of tasks that were the result of a big two-day meeting at the beginning of the year and has collected more dust than checkmarks. My honest response to the leader giving me this crazy strategic plan is, "You know, if everything is important, nothing is important."

Although this humongous plan might be acceptable with the larger organization, it is rarely such with teams (and even with smaller organizations and companies). It's difficult for a team to focus on the how, if the how feels overwhelming and even impossible. With such a big plan, by the end of the year the team feels deflated because only a handful of the goals, if even that, were actually completely realized—with the rest only partially or not realized at all. This becomes a perpetuating problem every year following because people know there won't be full closure on the strategic plan. Not having full closure is uninspiring. The plan becomes more of a once-a-year activity that people know won't mean much beyond that.

Strategic team plans need to be focused on three to five main things at the most, not 15 to 30. And strategic planning needs to become a process throughout the year, not a one-time event.

Main things are those goals that matter the most. They are the three to five most important things that if your team did them would help you get closer to realizing your vision. And bringing your team into defining what those three to five main things are makes the most sense because again, people buy in and support the things they help create.

Your team's strategic plan, much like the larger organization's plan, includes tasks, dates of when those tasks will be done, and who is responsible for completing each of them. However, different than most strategic plans, your strategic team plan is a living document. When one main thing is completed, you add another through the same process you went through to define the original three to five. You don't get together for a strategic planning session just once a year; a strategic team plan continues to be revisited, updated, massaged, and added to throughout the year as goals are completed and focuses change. You are going to approach your team's strategic planning as a process, not an event.

Pause, Reflect, and Apply

- Do you have a team strategic plan? If so, when is the last time you looked at it? Is your team inspired by it? How well does it align to your vision? If you don't have a strategic plan, then set some time aside soon and create one.

_____

_____

_____

You can get all of the free tools offered in this book, along with the Care to Lead Leader strategic team plan template, by going to www.doyoucaretolead.com/tools.

Individual Goals: Keep Your Eye on the Target (the Where) In a workforce study, only 30% of employees stated that they strongly agreed that their manager involved them in setting goals at work. And only 20% strongly agreed that they even had a conversation in the last six months with their manager about steps they could take in reaching their goals. However, those who were involved in goal setting at work were 3.6 times more engaged.[4]

I could have easily included this section on individual goals in chapter 3 on nurturing. Goal setting is a development and nurturing activity that Care to Lead Leaders are regularly engaged in with those they lead. But it is also an activity used to inspire people to big things and, importantly, aligns with teams that are creating a team vision, team purpose, and a strategic team plan.

Much like the strategic team plan, your people should have only three to five goals (and even less in some cases, depending on how involved the goals are). An individual goal document is also a living document. Similar to the strategic plan process, it too must be revisited, updated, massaged, and added to throughout the year as goals are completed and focuses change. A good time to revisit it is in every one-on-one or meeting you have. As a leader you are checking for goal alignment, goal progress or completion, obstacles (that you help remove if possible), and the impact and success the goals are having. This is not a two-times-a-year event where you set the goals and then evaluate the performance on individual goals at the end of the year. Revisiting goal documents as part of your one-on-ones with every person on your team should be happening at least once a month, if not more often, depending on the person. This is a nurturing activity that Care to Lead Leaders value as a critical process to inspiring and moving their people and teams to greater heights.

The following are some guidelines in helping you set goals with your people:

- **Align goals.** Every person you lead should have goals that link to the team strategic plan. People need to know how their success affects the team success and the overall success of the organization. When creating goals, that line to the team's plan should be clear, and a discussion on how their success is affecting the team and organization should be a regular part of every one-on-one. I call this the *success line*. Being able to draw a success line is not only a great opportunity to make a connection but also is big-time inspiring!

- **Aim high, but be realistic.** You are going to need strong individual goals from your team in order to fulfill the team's vision, but some goals aren't possible due to experience, resources, and time lines. Care to Lead Leaders are sensitive to these things. Failing to achieve an impossible goal can be demoralizing to those you lead. At the same time, the goals that are being set need to be challenging, most likely uncomfortable, and raise the bar for the individual as well as the team. If you are going to fulfill the team's dream (the vision), you are going to need goals that stretch people, because realizing dreams doesn't come without hard work and many times really difficult but not impossible work.

- **Make them measurable.** The only way to determine someone's success is through being able to measure their success. Simply saying "I will significantly improve my sales by such and such date" or "I will finish x, y, z project by this date" is not enough. This seems like a no-brainer, but I have worked with enough teams to tell you it isn't.

    Goals need to have some kind of indicator to measure their success; otherwise, it will be difficult to draw a success line. For example, I am going to finish x, y, z product in three months is easy to measure—you either finish the product or you don't. And yes, you finished the product, but what are the indicators that you successfully completed it. Hint: finishing it on time isn't one of them. You may have completed it, but the product may be horrible. Unfortunately, that is what happens with a lot of goals based on completing a project, a product, or a task. We are so focused on the completion, we forget to focus on a successful completion. What does a successful completion look like? That's something you need to discuss with your people. This applies to individual goals as well as your strategic team plan.

- **Clarify goals for understanding.** When done setting goals, make sure you clarify them. Is there an understanding of the goals, expectations about the goals, and knowledge of what success looks like when the goal has been achieved? Talk about each of these and make sure you are on the same page with those you lead.

- **Express confidence.** Care to Lead Leaders believe in those they lead, and those they lead know they believe in them. Regularly expressing this belief is hypercritical to your and your team's success. When setting goals with your people, express that you believe they can do this. Tell them that everyone is depending on each other's success to help the team's success. Let them know that they play an important role for the team and organization, again drawing that success line, and telling them, "You got this." *Note: If for some reason that feels forced and you don't believe they can do it, then you might need to adjust the goal or goals.*

- **Support.** In one study, only 3 in 10 US employees agreed that they had what they needed in terms of materials and equipment to do their job appropriately. And not having the materials and equipment needed to do their job well was found to be the greatest indicator, out of 12 total indicators, of stress.[5] If you really care about those you lead, you not only ensure they have the right materials and equipment but also one-on-one support as well. It is important that you express your support and that you are specific about what that support looks like. Your people need to know that you care enough to be there for whatever they need to be successful.

You can get a free Care to Lead Leader goal template to use with those that you lead by going to www.doyoucare tolead.com/tools.

Up Your Expectations

As it pertains to your team(s) and members of your team(s), what you expect can make the difference between rocket rides and subway rides. People rise to the level that others expect of them. Care to Lead Leaders know that those they lead have the ability to regularly have the bar raised. Even if those you lead initially don't believe the bar can be raised, your belief in them eventually gives them the confidence that it can be raised, and their new belief in themselves becomes a self-fulfilling prophecy. This is called the Pygmalion effect. People tend to live up or down to our expectations.

In the 1960s, Robert Rosenthal conducted a hallmark study with Lenore Jacobson at an elementary school in San Francisco.[6] The purpose of their study was to find out how teachers would react if they were told that a selection of students in their class had above-average academic potential. He labeled those students *bloomers*. The bloomers were selected randomly and on average were not any smarter than the rest of the students.

At the end of the year the children were given another IQ test as they had been given at the beginning of the year. The bloomers had shown significant increases in their IQ tests when compared to the other students. The expectations teachers had of these students had been realized.

Your people all have seeds of greatness within them. The only option of Care to Lead Leaders is to do everything they can to help that seed sprout and eventually become full grown. Part of nurturing and inspiring is raising the expectations we have of others. The higher our expectations are of others, and might I add, confidence and belief in others, the greater they will become.

It was once said, "Treat a man as he is and he will remain as he is. Treat a man as he could be and he will become what he should be."

Pause, Reflect, and Apply

- Are you setting high-enough expectations for your organization(s), team(s), and people? Is there anything you might change?

  _____

  _____

  _____

Positive Leaders Inspire Positive Results

In 2008 the US was in the midst of a really bad recession, second only to the Great Depression of the 1930s. I will never forget an experience I had while consulting with one particular highly dysfunctional senior leadership team. We were discussing some of the morale issues their staff members were having when one of the senior leaders said, "I don't think morale and motivating people really matters these days. Given the way things are people should just be lucky they have a job."

After picking my jaw up off the floor, I boldly responded, "You better think it matters because when this thing turns around [talking about the failed economy at the time], guess where your employees will be going: right out that door to your competitor!" It does matter, and it matters a lot. Great leaders' value and inspire those they lead through creating positive places of work. If they fail to value and inspire, those they lead will find other opportunities, and any good that has been built will go with them. The low morale in this company had less to do with the economy and much more to do with leaders like this. Negativity breeds negativity and anything less than a positive place to work will ensure people are regularly looking for another place to work. What positive energy are you bringing to your team and organization? Your influence as a Care to Lead Leader matters.

In my first book, *You Are the Team: 6 Simple Ways Teammates Can Go from Good to Great,* I shared the following reflective story.

In a remote Japanese village, there was a happy and energetic little puppy that heard of a place called the palace of 1,000 mirrors and decided to pay a visit. When he arrived, he playfully bounced up the steep stairs to the open door of the house. He entered the palace with his ears perked and his tail wagging very fast. To his surprise, this little puppy found 1,000 other happy puppies just like him, all of whom were also wagging their tails just as he was.

He gave a great big smile and found the other 1,000 dogs smiling right back, which made him smile even bigger. The bigger he smiled and the faster he wagged his tail, the more the other 1,000 puppies smiled and wagged their tails.

As he left the palace, he said to himself, "What a wonderful place! I must come back and visit again."

In the same village, there was an older and very grumpy puppy. He also decided to visit the palace of 1,000 mirrors. As he approached the door with his sad head hung low, he looked up and found 1,000 other grumpy and unhappy dogs staring back at him. He growled and was frightened by the other dogs that growled back at him. He quickly left and said to himself, "That place is dreadful and a bit terrifying. I won't ever go back again."

The moral of the story, of course, is that you get back what you reflect. Each of us lives in a different palace of 1,000 mirrors. Which palace you choose to spend the most time in depends on your choice to be positive or not. Even if everyone else around you is negative, you can make the choice to be positive instead. You have to become the change that you ultimately want to see. There are going to be times the palace you are in is going to need a major makeover, but that renovation starts with you as a Care to Lead Leader. If you want a team and organization of happy positive people, then you have to be happy and positive yourself. Most people want to be around people who are positive. In fact, even negative people want to be around positive people. Eventually it starts rubbing off. It's called *emotional contagion,* a "phenomenon of having one person's emotions and related behaviors directly trigger similar emotions and behaviors in other people."[7] There is a lot of research that backs this up.

In one study, researchers Emilio Ferrara of the University of Southern California and Zeyao Yang of Indiana University randomly selected 3,800 Twitter users. Using an algorithm that determined the emotional value of a tweet, they discovered that if a user had a higher than average number of positive tweets in their feed, they were more likely to put out positive tweets. And if users had a higher than average number of negative tweets, they were more likely to put out more negative tweets.[8] The research demonstrates that positive as well as negative emotions are contagious and transferred from one person to another.

In another study, researchers Fowler and Christakis, at Harvard Medical School and University of California, San Diego, respectively, explored the impact of friends on happiness and sadness looking at close to 5,000 people over a 20-year period. They found that when one person is happy, the effect can be measured up to three degrees. In other words, a chain reaction is triggered; when one person becomes happy that not only benefits one friend but also the friends of that friend and their friends' friends. The impact lasts up to one year![9]

Peter Totterdell at the University of Sheffield studied cricket teams (a sport somewhat similar to baseball). He found that when a team was positive and upbeat that the spirit of the team's overall good mood was transferred to individual players and those players believed that they played better than usual.[10] In another study, Moll, Jordet, and Pepping looked at the behavior of soccer players after a successful kick during the penalty shootout phase of a match. What they found was that teams who celebrated with certain behavior (big smiles, raising fists, etc.) with each other after a successful kick were most likely part of the winning team as opposed to those who didn't.[11]

Most people think twice about bringing germs into the office, but how often do we think about what we are spreading with our moods through emotional contagion? Those moods can be more toxic than germs. And leaders have the ability to bring high levels of mood toxicity to their organizations and teams if they aren't careful due to their larger influence on those they lead as a whole.

So, how do you improve your positivity as a Care to Lead Leader? You can start with smiling more, being kinder, and complimenting more often.

Smile The humanitarian and compassionate advocate for the poor Mother Teresa once said, "We shall never know all the good that a simple smile can do." Smiling is a powerful tool for creating positivity. There are many reasons to grin from ear to ear as a lot of research has affirmed. Smiling relieves stress, makes you happier, improves mental health, decreases heart rate and blood pressure, makes you feel younger and more attractive, increases your chances of success, helps you live longer, and can even make you look thinner—forget the diet programs, right?

How often we smile might surprise you? Children smile about 400 times a day and adults who are in a good mood smile 40 to 50 times, but usually adults on average only smile about 20 times a day.[12] Would you agree we could all smile more?

Smiling has the same effects as service, as discussed when we talked about the service effect. When you smile your brain is throwing a mood-enhancing, feel-good party! Dopamine, endorphins, and serotonin are released when you smile and when you see someone else smile. In fact, I challenge you to look at a picture of someone smiling and try to frown. Although you can force yourself to frown, it feels like a bit of a contradiction. In a Swedish study, research participants were presented with pictures of people expressing different emotions. When the picture of someone smiling was shown, researchers asked participants to frown. People had a hard time not imitating what they were seeing.[13] It took a conscious effort on the participant's part to switch from a smile to a frown.

Smiling is contagious. We can't help but smile back when someone smiles at us and it feels good. Next time someone smiles at you and you smile back, be aware of how it makes you feel. Because our moods improve as we smile, the moods of others also improve. Care to Lead Leaders understand the power of smiling in inspiring and creating positivity where they lead.

Pause, Reflect, and Apply

- Take a smile break once or several times a day for five minutes or so. Walk the halls and floors of where you lead and just look people in the eyes and smile. Not only is this going to improve how you feel, as we discussed, but also it is going to have a direct impact on those you are smiling at. Encourage others to take smile breaks as well.

  _____

  _____

  _____

Be Kind There is no training program that teaches it. The skills of strategic planning, organization, sharp decision-making, and delegation don't require it. But every Care to Lead Leader possesses it. What is it? It's kindness. You have probably had a leader, as I have, who was self-centered, thoughtless, lacked manners, and was rude. How did that work for you? Although such leaders can get results, they are only going to get just enough from people so that they don't get a crossed look or a rude comment.

Being kind to others doesn't hurt. It doesn't take much time, it's actually quite simple, and it's always the right thing to do. A number of years ago Gayle LaSalle, CEO at LaSalle Consulting and Training, shared a story on my blog. It's a simple lesson in kindness. She said:

> I've found it amazing how a simple "thank you" can go a long way. So can a heartfelt "you're welcome!"
>
> A few years ago, I was having lunch with my 3-year-old granddaughter and her mom. She has been taught to say thank you when someone does something for you. She said "thank you" to the waiter, who simply walked away. She looked at her mom and said, "He didn't say you're welcome." If a 3-year-old notices, you can be sure others do as well.

Care to Lead Leaders put kindness at the center of everything they do. Doing so improves trust, respect, commitment, and loyalty. Kind leaders also encourage and then see the spread of kindness on their team(s) and in their organization(s). Nobel Peace Prize recipient Aung San Suu Kyi once beautifully said in her award speech, 21 years after receiving it due to being a political prisoner during much of that time:

> Of the sweets of adversity, and let me say that these are not numerous, I have found the sweetest, the most precious of all, is the lesson I learnt on the value of kindness. Every kindness I received, small or big, convinced me that there could never be enough of it in our world. To be kind is to

respond with sensitivity and human warmth to the hopes and needs of others. Even the briefest touch of kindness can lighten a heavy heart. Kindness can change the lives of people.[14]

Kindness creates positive workplaces. Kindness inspires others to do their greatest work. Kindness can indeed change lives.

Pause, Reflect, and Apply

- How kind are you to those you lead? How would those you lead respond to that question? What will you change as a result?

_____

_____

_____

Compliment Complimenting is one of the fastest ways to create positive energy on your teams and in your organizations. However, studies show it isn't happening enough. A Gallup Poll found that only 3 out of 10 employees on average had received praise or recognition for doing a good job at work in the last seven days. The researchers stated that by moving that ratio from 3 in 10 to 6 in 10 organizations could see a 24% improvement in quality, a 27% reduction in absenteeism, and 10% reduction in shrinkage.[15] Taking the time to compliment others can result in big-time benefits.

Care to Lead Leaders consistently, personally, specifically, succinctly, and genuinely provide praise and recognition. Doing so raises the level of loyalty and focus on results with those you lead.

- **Consistently.** Consistency is the key to complimenting others. Give too few, and you are going to fail to reap the benefits. Give too many, and compliments are going to begin to lose their value because they feel insincere.

- **Personally.** Understanding what people like to be complimented on makes a difference. Think about what people value the most in terms of compliments. Make it personal.

- **Specifically.** Instead of simply saying, "You are a great project leader," be specific and say instead, "I really like how detailed you are when you lead a project. Because of your detail to this project we were able to avoid several potential costly mistakes."

- **Succinctly.** Too many details or too many gushy positive affirmations in one interaction can have the same effect as giving too many compliments—it starts to lose its value. You don't want a compliment to feel overwhelming.

- **Genuinely.** Everything you do as a Care to Lead Leader needs to be genuine. If you aren't feeling it from the heart, you shouldn't say it. People will feel your compliment as trite or fake if not given from the heart.

Mark Twain once said, "I can live for two months on a good compliment."[16] My experience is that I have lived on many good compliments much longer than that. Compliments and recognition throughout my life has in many cases shaped who I am today. A good leader can influence your life through what they do and what they say. If you rarely take the time to see the good in others, very few will see the good in you. And if you don't take the time to compliment others, you will rarely get a compliment in return and believe me, leaders need their share of compliments as well, as you probably know.

Complimenting, similar to many of the things we have discussed in this chapter, is contagious. There are a number of ways you can help your team spread it. One easy thing that leaders and teams I have worked with have found helpful is to spend some time in a meeting having people share one positive thing about every person in the room. It could be something they recently did that helped someone or simply an attribute, gift, or talent that they have that makes everyone better. You might choose to do this quarterly or biannually, or in a regular team meeting when you just focus on one person at a time. I have found that leaders who do this create amazing positive energy on their team. You can't help but be inspired when not only the leader is consistently complimenting but your team as well!

Choose to be a bucket filler, not a bucket dipper. Bucket fillers inspire others through the thoughtful and positive things they say about others. We all need our buckets at full capacity.

Pause, Reflect, and Apply

- Are you complimenting enough? Are your compliments consistent, personal, specific, succinct, and genuine?

  _____

  _____

  _____

- Complimenting is an act of service, similar to many of the actions that I cover in this book. I shared a story in chapter 1 on service about a CEO who put a handful of marbles in his pocket at the beginning of each day. When he paid someone a specific, genuine compliment, he would then transfer one marble to the other pocket. His goal each night was to set a handful of transferred marbles on his night stand and start all over the next day. If you feel you aren't complimenting enough, or that your compliments are not of the quality they should be, start with a pocket of marbles each day. When you have paid a compliment, and it has met the criteria of a good compliment, then transfer that marble to your other pocket.

  _____

  _____

  _____

Recognition and Rewards

In a 10-year, 200,000-person study, 65% of North American employees stated that they failed to be recognized even once the previous year.[17] That number is astounding to me; how about you? It means that only 35% of employees are being recognized at all. I have to think that even less than that receive rewards. Recognition, which can include a wide range of actions, seems like such a no-brainer, but obviously it is overlooked by a majority of leaders even though global studies show that recognition is the number one thing leaders can give their employees to inspire them to greater work.[18]

A big opportunity for you as a Care to Lead Leader is to inspire your people by providing the right types of recognition and rewards. It's not a checklist item: you must be careful and thoughtful in how you do it.

One of the things I have always enjoyed in the small town I live in is the parades. In fact, as I write this, we have a big one tomorrow. At these parades participants on the floats throw out candy. It is always interesting to watch the behavior of people whenever something is thrown out for free. Kids are jumping out in front of bikes, floats, horses, and cars, risking limb and their lives on a piece of penny candy. Their parents are often times out there with them protecting their children with one hand and pushing other kids out of the way to fill up their bag with the other hand. It's quite the scene and a great study in human behavior.

However, the excitement often begins to wane after the first group of floats has passed and the same cheap candy has been thrown out over and over again. In fact, when the parade finishes, you can go down the street and pick up quite a few pieces of taffy and other penny candies still in their wrapper.

How does penny candy at a parade lose its value so quickly? First, when the candy is initially flying off the floats, people are incentivized to risk a lot of things because it seems exciting and rewarding. But they quickly realize that with so much being thrown, it doesn't take much to fill their bag with cheap candy. At that point they don't care about their now unexciting initial goal anymore and they stop trying as hard. Are the recognition and rewards you are giving the result of little effort and little achievements? If they are, those you lead may soon not care about their goals either. Although they may initially care and be excited at first, if your team goals and their personal goals are uninspiring and the recognition and rewards are easily achievable, what incentive do they have in the following months and years to achieve greater things than they ever achieved before? Very little.

Second, because so many types of candy are available at stores, including the delights of chocolate (not usually thrown out at parades), people quickly realize how boring penny candy really is and fail to care anymore. Are you dangling a big enough carrot in front of your people? Are you even dangling the right carrot? The reward of money, for example, might seem like a fairly big carrot, but there are many studies that show that cash is not at the top in terms of motivating people. In fact, things like gift cards or a gift selection from a catalog are more of an incentive than cold hard cash for many people. Money just gets spent on things like bills, gas and groceries, and feels impersonal in addition to being fleeting. It can also become an expectation more than a reward. For many, it simply fails to be the right carrot.

You may also fail to have the right carrot as it pertains to recognition. For example, some leaders love to recognize those they lead in public, in front of the entire team or organization. Although some people thrive on this type of recognition, others find it highly embarrassing. What could motivate one person could easily frustrate and de-incentivize another.

In chapter 3, I warned you about cookie cutter management because people are unique. If you want to reap the benefits of recognition and rewards, don't cookie cut recognition and rewards. Carefully think through how you recognize and reward those you lead, so that you can bring more positive energy to your team and inspire your people.

Pause, Reflect, and Apply

- How are you currently recognizing and rewarding those you lead? Do you think through how you are going to do it carefully? Find out how each person on your team likes to be recognized and rewarded. You can ask in your one-on-ones or simply send out a survey.

———————————————

———————————————

———————————————

Celebrate, Celebrate, Celebrate

How did you feel the last time someone celebrated some-thing you did well? Celebrating a success, whether that be a team's success or a team member's success, is one of those things Care to Lead Leaders do because they understand that it makes others feel good to be valued and appreciated. Celebrating is a close relative to recognition, but it has more of a congratulatory party feel to it and everyone is invited to feel good.

Leadership author and friend of mine Mark Macy tells the following story of a special celebration experience we can all learn from that he had with a basketball team he was asked to coach and a player affectionately referred to as *Bookworm:*

> My phone rang; it was a call from the Parks and Recreation Department asking me to coach a fifth-grade girls' basket-ball team. After a short discussion, I found out it was a "left-over" group of six girls from several schools that didn't get put on a team because the league had already filled all of their team rosters.
>
> Anyone who has coached knows that it takes at least five decent players, plus a couple of "stars," to win some games. The Parks and Rec leader informed me that with this team, the season would be a long one. He also said to not feel bad if we did not win a single game. "Just make sure they all get to play in each game," he said.
>
> As part of our discussion, I convinced the Parks and Rec department to allow me to recruit at least one addi-tional player so I could start the season with seven players.

Two of the seven had actually played before, four knew what a basketball was, and the other one had parents who had made her join as a way for her get out to expand her experiences. For lack of a better name, I will refer to this last player as *Bookworm*.

We began practice at a local gym a couple of times a week, starting with the basics and working up to a very simple defense and offense. We even learned an in-bounds play (getting the ball from outside the line of play and into the court).

As we practiced, I could tell that Bookworm was having a very difficult time. Her basketball skills were primitive at best. She couldn't shoot the ball high enough from any point on the floor to hit the net, let alone go through the basket. Her mother actually came up to me in private and asked what she could do to help her outside of practice. I gave her some very simple drills to try, thinking that at the very least they could keep her from getting hurt on the court when she did get to play.

Soon enough, the first game came. By some miracle, we actually won by a couple of points. We went on to win four in a row! In each of those games, I had been crafty in how much I let Bookworm play. I tried to hide her from a lot of interaction, trying to keep any potential embarrassment to a minimum.

I knew that there would be a game where Bookworm would actually get her hands on a ball, and if she touched the ball, a foul would likely be called. At that point, Bookworm would go to the line and eventually be humiliated because she couldn't even lift the ball higher than four feet. I could not let that happen.

As a solution, I focused on just having her shoot free throws practice after practice. I finally figured out that having her shoot "granny style" (shooting under the hands as opposed to on top of the hands) might be the only way to lift the ball high enough to at least get it close to the rim.

The game finally came where Bookworm got a rebound, and, you guessed it, she was fouled. The referee signaled two shots and showed her where the shooting line was. Her little legs and hands were shaking, her head was down, and she was scared to death. I called time-out.

As she stood there in the huddle, I clutched her hands to keep them from trembling and expressed my belief that she was going to do just great. I reminded her about the many hours of practice she had, and we reviewed what she had learned about shooting "granny style." Her teammates expressed confidence in her. The huddle broke, and she went back to the free throw line. It appeared that she was not as nervous, but she definitely did not have the swagger of a person who knows they will make the shot.

As she set up and launched her shot, I prayed, "God, let it please hit the rim!" The ball rose up and up and, to my surprise, even past the height of the net. Then the miracle occurred: the ball went right in—nothing but net. Swish!

She was shocked! The crowd went crazy! I stood there in disbelief. I called time-out again! Why? So we could celebrate as a team and enjoy the moment together. All season, we had worked hard and were fortunate to have celebrated in many team successes. Now, it was time to bask and celebrate in Bookworm's success. A miracle like this might not ever happen again.

The story doesn't end there. She then went back to the line for her second shot. This time, she wasn't dragging her feet or had her head down; instead, she walked with a swagger of confidence I've never seen from her. She took the ball, went through the same routine, and she ripped the ball through the hoop a second time!

I called a time-out again! Why? So, we could celebrate again! Those were the only two points Bookworm made that year.

Celebrating matters! Whether it's a personal, group, team, or organization celebration—celebrate! The story above demonstrates what the power of a compassionate, sensitive, and caring leader can have on someone and the influence they can have on a team when a time-out is called. Samuel Goldwyn, a Jewish Polish American film producer, put it this way: "When someone does something well, applaud! You will make two people happy."[19]

Pause, Reflect, and Apply

- How much celebration do you do as a team? Who do you have the opportunity to call a time-out for and celebrate?

_____

_____

_____

Thank You!

Similar to celebrating, another close relative of recognition is gratitude. People are inspired, feel more valued, and are more positive by gratitude. A study done by Glassdoor, an online career site, found that 81% of employees said they are inspired to work harder when their boss shows appreciation. Compare that to 38% who said they work harder when their boss is demanding and only 37% work harder when they fear losing a job.[20] Care to Lead Leaders know the value of "thank you" and regularly look for opportunities to say it.

An old story is told of a waiter who asked a customer how he had enjoyed the meal. The guest replied that it was fine, but he would have enjoyed it more if he had been given more bread. When the man came back for dinner the next evening, the waiter had doubled the amount of bread, giving him four large slices instead of two, but the man still wasn't happy. The next day, the bread was doubled again, without success.

On the fourth day the waiter was very determined to make sure the man walked away happy. He got a nine-foot loaf of bread, cut it in half and served it to the man. The waiter was so excited to see the man's reaction.

After the meal, the man looked up at the waiter and said, "Good as always. But I see you are back to giving only two slices of bread."

It is easy to get caught up in not seeing all that others do for us. For example, an employee who stays a little later to meet a deadline, a coworker who has spent 20 extra minutes helping solve a problem for a teammate, or someone on the team who always volunteers to do the things no one else volunteers to do. Are you noticing? Are you expressing gratitude? Who are the best leaders you have ever had? There is a good chance that they made thankfulness a regular practice of their leadership. They saw that you weren't simply back to giving two slices of bread.

Gratitude can be expressed formally with recognition. Or it can be expressed informally through a one-to-one personal statement or a note or a token of appreciation such as a small gift—which usually includes a personal statement or note. The key is to just do it however you choose to do it.

Regularly expressing gratitude to others requires that you are regularly looking for the positive things others are doing for you, the team, and the organization. When thankfulness is at the top of your mind, expressing it becomes a top priority. Here are some tips to help you to put more emphasis and create a greater awareness on gratitude:

- **Count blessings at bedtime.** Instead of counting sheep, count blessings. It cured my occasional insomnia at one time! Instead of worrying about everything you didn't get done and worrying about everything you have to get done, try focusing just on those things and people you are grateful for. All of the negative thoughts disappear. It works and you will wake up happier, too!

- **Take a gratitude walk.** Much like the smile break previously suggested, quietly take a moment to notice those around you as you walk the halls and floors for a minute or two. Reflect on how they make your day easier and why each of them is a blessing.

169
Inspire

- **Create a gratitude board.** Use a whiteboard with magnets to post picture of things you are grateful for. You can also use markers to write around pictures you have posted and why you are grateful for those particular things. Pictures can include family, team(s), employees, bosses, projects, products, events, and so on. It becomes something that you can reflect on at different points during the day. And imagine how your team would feel seeing a picture of themselves front and center on the board.

- **Take a moment to reflect.** At the start of each day think of 5 to 10 things you are grateful for. Close your eyes and picture them in your mind and feel the feelings in your body for each of them. You will begin to feel happier and happier every time you take the time to feel gratitude.

- **Send daily notes.** Create a habit every day of sending at least one handwritten note of appreciation. Each day, this is going to require you to reflect on one or several people you are grateful for. Over time this will become a positive habit that will shower positive energy to everyone around you.

How you express gratitude is a lot like how you give a compliment. It must be consistent, personal, specific, succinct, and expressed from your heart—genuine.

Appreciation is a leadership principle so basic, yet unfortunately so often neglected. It's simply about having a heart of thankfulness. Those leaders who have a heart of gratitude will also have the heart of those they lead. Warren Buffet, the highly successful billionaire investor and business leader, once wisely said that if you praised and appreciated people for the little things, they would give you bigger things to praise and appreciate later on.

Pause, Reflect, and Apply

- How often do you express gratitude? Would your team agree it is enough? Are you regularly and intentionally looking for opportunities when you can express gratitude? Make a commitment now to start using at least one of the tips today.

_____

_____

_____

Walk the Talk

You are going to find it very difficult to inspire if you say one thing but do another. Care to Lead Leaders not only inspire by what they say (more on that coming) but also by who they are and what they do. Expecting those you lead to have a strong work ethic, honor commitments, and have integrity won't be realized unless you also work hard, keep your promises, and are absolutely true and honest in all things. You can scream what you expect until you are blue in the face, but until you live it yourself it won't ever have much of an affect. Leaders who inspire by what they do and who they are change people, teams, and organizations.

Side-by-Side by Example

The story is told of a battlefield over 200 years ago, where a man in civilian clothes rode past a small group of tired and battled weary soldiers. They were trying to raise a beam to a high position.

The leader of the group wasn't making any effort to help. He just shouted words of support to no avail and then threatened the group if they didn't finish the work quickly.

"Why aren't you helping?" the stranger asked on horseback.

"I'm in charge! The men do as I tell them," said the leader. He added, "Help them yourself if you feel so strongly about it."

To the mean leader's surprise, the stranger got off his horse and helped the men until the job was finished. Before he left, the stranger congratulated the men for their work and approached the confused leader.

He said, "Next time you need help, call on me, your commander-in-chief, and I will come."

Up close, the now-humbled leader recognized General George Washington. He was taught a lesson that he would never forget!

I have always loved leaders who are willing to roll up their sleeves and work hard side-by-side with their teams. I have learned important lessons from those leaders, the most important being that they really cared. They not only said they cared but also demonstrated they cared by their actions. They walked the talk.

It's about How You Make Them Feel

Mayo Angelou, an American poet and civil rights activist, once said, "I've learned that people will forget what you said, people will forget what you did, but people will never forget how you made them feel."[21] How you make others feel is a differentiator of Care to Lead Leaders. If people feel good around you, they are going to want to be around you because they are inspired by you. If people feel bad around you, they are going to want to avoid you because they aren't inspired by you. That's the price you pay as a leader who fails to walk the talk. There are other prices to be paid as well.

You have probably seen leaders who for example say something like "customers always come first," but then fail to hire enough staff to handle the number of calls growing each day. Or the leader who says "during this busy season, we must all work harder and longer," and then takes a scheduled holiday trip with his family. Or, the leader who says "teamwork is vitally important to our organization," but fails to remove obstacles and is often the very cause of challenges that prevent teams from working together. These "say one thing and do another thing" leaders quickly lose trust and people become less engaged over time, less receptive to new ideas, and in general less willing to follow those that lead when the talk doesn't include the walk.

Do What You Say You Will Do

Often times failing to walk the talk includes not honoring commitments or promises you have made to people.

A promise is a promise, right? But in many cases leaders fail to honor those promises. I am sure you have had leaders who break their word. Did you feel any different about that leader? Every time a leader breaks a promise or fails to live up to a commitment, little by little those they lead believe less of what they say. They tune out, roll their eyes, and talk to others about failed promises and commitments of the past. We let a lot of people down when we fail to honor our word.

Be realistic. If you can't do something, don't commit to it or promise to do it. I have found there are three kinds of people when it comes to doing what you say you will do. There's those who do it (we all love those people), there's those who don't, and there's those who can't say no. If you are in the third group, learn to say no, but find a way to help the requestor get it done. Maybe you can do it at a later date, or maybe you know someone else who could help, or maybe the requestor just needs confidence to know he or she can do it. Care to Lead Leaders are transparent and honest about what they can and can't do, but at the very least they always find a way to help somehow.

Have Personal Integrity

If you fail in personal integrity you fail every person you lead. Walking the talk in terms of living up to the values of your organization and society as a whole isn't just important but absolutely, hands-down, critical. Integrity is the cornerstone of leadership. And it's a large enough cornerstone that if it is compromised, it usually can't be repaired. Certainly, you can be successful by lying, deceiving, and being dishonest in general, but it is a short-term game. Sooner or later people see right through it all and you become not only less effective as a leader but also not very popular.

Pause, Reflect, and Apply

- Take careful inventory of how you walk the talk. Honestly ask yourself how you are doing with each of the principles just described. If your team were asked, how would they say you are doing?

  _____

  _____

  _____

Talk the Walk

It is important to walk the talk, but Care to Lead Leaders also talk the walk. They understand the importance of inspiring communication in their day-to-day interaction with those they lead whether that be a one-on-one discussion or a presentation to an entire organization. You can't expect visions to be realized, purposes to be embraced, and goals to be completed if you can't inspire those you lead through regular and strong communication. Doing communication right adds more of the right ingredients to the formula and fuel to the rocket.

When I work with teams, communication is often cited as the number one obstacle, right next to trust. I have always believed that one inhibits the other. When communication is poor, trust suffers. When trust suffers, communication tends to get worse. And leaders who fail to communicate effectively and regularly consequently lose the trust of those they lead.

One night an angry man and wife were preparing for bed. Neither of them had spoken to each other most of the night.

It was normal for the couple to boil in a war of silence for several days. However, this time the man was concerned because he needed to be woken up at 5:00 AM the next morning so that he could catch an important flight. He was a heavy sleeper and relied on his wife to wake him up; otherwise, there was a good chance he would sleep right through the alarm!

Letting his pride get the best of him he cleverly decided he would write her a note while she was in the bathroom instead of asking her verbally. He wrote on the piece of paper: "Please wake me up at 5:00 AM. I have a critical flight to catch." He put the note on his wife's pillow believing she would for sure see it there. He then tucked himself in and went to bed.

The next morning when he woke up, he looked at the clock, and it was 7:00 AM! He was enraged that he had missed his flight and was preparing to go up the stairs and give his errant wife a scolding when he noticed a handwritten note on his nightstand.

The note said: "It's 5:00 AM—get up."

Although this is funny in a kind of sad way, it highlights where communication often fails. Care to Lead Leaders know that inspiring others means delivering the best message in the best way, which is about choosing the right medium, rehearsing what you are communicating in person, using stories to draw people in, and committing to consistently communicate.

Choosing the Right Medium

Care to Leaders carefully choose the medium they plan to deliver their message with. I once consulted with a CEO who loved the written word when she communicated with her organization. Rarely did she deliver important messages to the larger organization in person; instead, she chose to write long, carefully crafted messages delivered via email or care-fully bounded documents. She spent hours working on them, but they failed, for the most part, in resonating and connecting with people. Unfortunately, I came to understand that jokes were often made around the office about her long-winded letters and how like a hermit she was held up in her office creating the next "big surprise." Her time would have been much better spent in outlining, practicing, and delivering the message in person and where everyone was present and peo-ple could ask questions. Does that mean you shouldn't ever communicate by written word? Of course not. But like any communication, it can't be your only medium. You have to find out what is best for the situation.

Rehearsing What You Are Communicating in Person

As a speaker, I know the value of rehearsing. I spend hours preparing and rehearsing for keynotes and workshops I deliver. Why? Because I want to deliver a message that has a real lasting, practical, and actionable impact on the people I am speaking to. As a leader of teams and large organizations in my past, I used to do the same thing. I focused on making sure that the message was clear, articulate, and could be delivered in a way that inspired. But as I have worked with many leaders, very few are taking the time to do the same. Why? Because they either don't know about the power of rehearsing what they communicate, or they just don't care.

I hope it's not the latter. Over the years I have rehearsed hundreds of important communications while preparing to deliver them. It didn't matter if it was a big organization, large or small team, or even one-on-ones; every communication was important, and I knew it was important to those I was delivering it to. Finding the time to do it was a priority. I have rehearsed in cars driving home, in my offices, and even in the shower; I always found the time to do it. Rehearsing has helped me get the message right and the confidence to deliver it well. It's enabled me to anticipate and answer any questions that might come up as well.

Some people fear speaking in front of groups—small and large—more than death. And I would fear it at that level as well if I didn't take the time necessary in rehearsal. You won't inspire those you lead if you fail to effectively communicate with poise, confidence, and energy, which comes from the way it sounds and the way it looks as you deliver your message. Rehearsing that message is the key.

Using Stories to Draw People In

Next time you attend a conference or meeting where a presentation is being delivered, look around the room. When a story is told, look around the room again. People quickly go from checking their phones, looking at anything besides the speaker, and not looking very interested in general to all of sudden putting their phones down, looking at the speaker, and looking really interested. I have watched this time and time again. If a story is being told, people pay attention.

Personal stories always go over well in communication, especially those that show some vulnerability on your part as we talked about way back in chapter 2. There are a variety of stories you can use if you look. They can be fictional stories, news stories, inspiring true stories, a story that happened to someone you know, or even fables and parables similar to some of the ones I have shared in this book. The important thing is that you make a choice to tell stories and that you tell the right stories to inspire those that you lead.

I suggest getting in the habit of telling stories when you communicate. Try to include at least one story in every message you deliver. If the message is longer, include two or more. I would also suggest that you create a story file that contains all the great stories you collect so you always have them readily available. Stories are inspiring and make a genuine impact on those you lead.

Committing to Consistently Communicate

Being inconsistent in your communication is almost as bad as failing to communicate at all. When communication is infrequent, and especially if you are out of site, people begin to create their own stories. The stories created because of your absence of communication are not the kind you want shared. Caring leaders communicate frequently, openly, and as transparently as possible.

- How well are you talking the walk? How can you improve the quality and frequency of your communication? If your team was asked how well you communicate, what would they say?

_____

_____

_____

Care to Lead Leader Inspire Takeaways

- Care to Lead Leaders have a clear team what (vision), team why (purpose), and personal and team how (goals).

- Those you lead will rise to the level of your expectations.

- Positive leaders contagiously create positive teams and in turn positive results.

- Rewards and recognition can either incentivize when done right or de-incentivize when done wrong.

- Calling time-outs and regularly celebrating people and teams inspires and helps others feel good, valued, and appreciated.

- Those leaders who have a heart of gratitude will also have the heart of those they lead.

- Regularly expressing gratitude to others requires that you are regularly looking for the positive things others are doing for you, your team, and your organization.

- Expecting those you lead to have a strong work ethic, honor commitments, and have integrity won't be realized unless you also work hard, keep your promises, and are absolutely true and honest in all things. Simply walk the talk.

- You can't expect visions to be realized, purposes to be embraced, and goals to be completed if you can't inspire those you lead through regular and strong communication.

Notes

1. Jane Carruth, adapter; Lewis Carroll, *Alice in Wonderland* (New York: Gramercy Books 2004). (Originally published in 1865.)
2. Gallup, *State of the American Workplace* (Washington, DC: Gallup Inc., 2017), 80.
3. Linda Hill and Kent Lineback, "The Fundamental Purpose of Your Team," *Harvard Business Review,* Last modified July 12, 2011, https://hbr.org/2011/07/the-fundamental-purpose-of-you.html.

4. Gallup, *State of the American Workplace*, 79, 80.

5. Ibid., 102.

6. R. Rosenthal and L. Jacobson, "Teachers' Expectancies: Determinants of Pupils' IQ Gains," *Psychological Reports* 19 (1966): 115–118.

7. Wikipedia, "Emotional Contagion," *Wikipedia, The Free Encyclopedia,* https://en.wikipedia.org/w/index.php?title=Emotional_contagion&oldid=902302049.

8. Emilio Ferrara and Zeyao Yang, "Measuring Emotional Contagion in Social Media," *PLoS One* 10, no. 11: e0142390.

9. James H. Fowler and Nicholas A. Christakis, "Dynamic Spread of Happiness in a Large Social Network: Longitudinal Analysis over 20 Years in the Framingham Heart Study," *British Medical Journal* (December 4, 2008).

10. P. Totterdell, "Catching Moods and Hitting Runs: Mood Linkage and Subjective Performance in Professional Sport Teams," *Journal of Applied Psychology* 85, no. 6: 848–59.

11. Tjerk Moll, Geir Jordet, and Jan-Gert Pepping, "Emotional Contagion in Soccer Penalty Shootouts: Celebration of Individual Success Is Associated with Ultimate Team Success," *Journal of Sports Sciences* 28, no. 9: 983–92.

12. Earlexia Norwood, "Surprising Health Benefits of Smiling.," *Henry Ford Health System*. Last modified October 5, 2017, https://www.henryford.com/blog/2017/10/health-benefits-smiling.

13. Ronald E. Riggio, "There's Magic in Your Smile.," *Psychology Today,* Last modified June 25, 2012, https://www.psychologytoday.com/us/blog/cutting-edge-leadership/201206/there-s-magic-in-your-smile.

14. Peter Popham, "Aung San Suu Kyi: A Lesson in the Value of Kindness," *Independent,* Last modified June 17, 2012.

https://www.independent.co.uk/news/world/asia/aung-
san-suu-kyi-a-lesson-in-the-value-of-kindness-7856643
.html.

15. Gallup, *State of the American Workplace,* 106.

16. Albert Bigelow Paine, *Mark Twain, a Biography: The
Personal and Literary Life of Samuel Langhorne Clemens*
(Vol. IV) (New York: Harper & Brothers Publishers, 1912),
1334.

17. OC Tanner Learning Group, "Performance Accelerated,"
n.d., https://www.octanner.com/content/dam/oc-
tanner/documents/global-research/White_Paper_
Performance_Accelerated.pdf.

18. David Stuart and Todd Nordstrom, "10 Shocking
Workplace Stats You Need to Know," *Forbes,* Last
modified March 8, 2018, https://www.forbes.com/sites/
davidsturt/2018/03/08/10-shocking-workplace-stats-
you-need-to-know.

19. Ed McClements, "Financial Sources of Funds During a
Critical Illness," *LinkedIn,* January 25, 2016, https://www
.linkedin.com/pulse/financial-sources-funds-during-
critical-illness-ed.

20. Michael Schneider, "Employees Say This 1 Thing Would
Make Them Work Harder (And 6 Reasons Why Managers
Won't Do It)," Last modified December 28, 2017, https://
www.inc.com/michael-schneider/employees-say-this-1-
thing-would-make-them-work-harder-and-6-reasons-
why-managers-wont-do-it.html.

21. Maya Angelou, "The Quote Archive," *Tiny Buddha,*
https://tinybuddha.com/wisdom-quotes/ive-learned-
that-people-will-forget-what-you-said-people-will-
forget-what-you-did-but-people-will-never-forget-how-
you-made-them-feel/.

Chapter 5

Commit

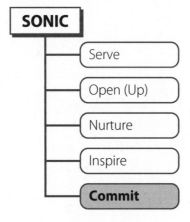

There's no turning back to old habits or old ways. You are now forging new habits and new ways.

There is a legend told of Captain Hernán Cortés, who in 1519 had landed in Veracruz with his 500 soldiers and 100 sailors on 11 ships. They were there to conquer an army much bigger than theirs that was holding on to the world's greatest treasures. These riches contained gold, silver, jewels, and artifacts that had been held by this army for 600 years. Everyone knew about this treasure, and army after army had tried to take it unsuccessfully.

Some of Cortés's men were not convinced that they would be successful and tried to seize ships and go to Cuba. To ensure that there were no other opportunities to retreat and that his men were completely invested and committed to the conquest and treasure, Cortés told them to sink and destroy all of their ships. His men resisted, wondering how they would get back home. He told them, "When we go home, we are going home on their ships!" There was no turning back; they either conquered, or they died. They conquered. In 600 years, no one else was able to do what they had done. But no one else had taken the measures to commit as Cortés and his army had.

Commitment to Becoming a Care to Lead Leader

In order for you to become a Care to Lead Leader you have to completely commit. This fifth part of the formula is poured and mixed from the beginning of your quest to be a Care to Lead Leader and continues to be poured and mixed as long as you lead. If you aren't completely committed to the first four parts of the formula (service, opening up, nurturing, and inspiring), which are really about committing to lead from the heart, you will ultimately fail to make your Care to Lead Leadership work.

Commitment is the binding agent that holds the rest of the formula together. You have to be committed to your team and organization and yourself. There's no turning back to old habits or old ways; you are now forging new habits and new ways. A one-day or even a one-month, six-month or one-year commitment to become a new and better leader is not enough; you have to be completely in and make a choice to sink and destroy your old ships. That starts with your commitment to your own personal development from here on out.

Pause, Reflect, and Apply

- On a scale of 1 to 10, with 10 being the highest, how committed are you to becoming a Care to Lead Leader?

  _____

  _____

  _____

Growth Is Not Optional

When I first started traveling years ago, there was one piece of safety instruction that had initially confused me when I had heard it for the first time. Those of you that travel regularly will recognize it. Over the speaker the flight attendant would say, *In case there is a sudden drop in pressure in the main cabin, oxygen masks will drop … If you are flying with a small child or with someone who might need assistance, put your oxygen mask on first, then assist them with theirs.*

I asked myself at that time, *why would I put my mask on first instead of helping someone else first? That is the selfish and cowardly thing to do! I must serve others first.* But then it of course dawned on me that if I heroically helped others without securing my mask, it would only be a matter of seconds before I wouldn't be good for anyone else, including myself! I would simply run out of oxygen and pass out.

Similar to the oxygen mask, if you fail to spend time on and commit to personal development and self-care such as personal health, rest, and relaxation, you are likely to run out of air as well. When you run out of air, you won't be much good to anyone. Not only do you need to recharge your batteries but also you need to replace them from time to time with bigger and better batteries

There is an old proverb that refers to "the one that makes shoes goes barefoot." Or in other words, everyone has shoes, except for the shoemaker. Chances are many on your team(s) and in your organization(s) are getting development, except you. I have seen in my experience that many leaders believe personal development is a priority when asked but fail to actually make it a priority. I want to challenge you first to make a commitment to personally put the shoes of Care to Lead Leadership on your feet with the plan on keeping them on for the long term. Second, I want to challenge you to do personal development the right way. Don't let it, including what you have learned in this book, become a five-minute university.

The Five-Minute University

One of my favorite videos of all time is an old comedy skit by former "Saturday Night Live" character Father Guido Sarducci. He was offering what he called the *five-minute university*. The idea was that in five minutes you would learn "what the average college graduate remembers five years after he or she is out of school." Tuition would only be 20 dollars, which included the tuition, a cap and gown rental, a graduation picture, and everything else you needed. As part of this university, similar to many others, a foreign language would be a requirement. But at the five-minute university you can take any language you want. If you are taking Spanish for example, Sarducci says, what he teaches you is, *¿cómo está usted,* which means "how are you," and the answer is *muy bien,* which means, "very well." Sarducci says "believe me if you took two years of college Spanish, five years after you get out of school, *¿cómo está usted* and *muy bien* are about all you are to going to remember." "So, in my school," he says, "that's all they learn. You see, you don't have to waste your time with conjugations, vocabulary, all that junk. You just forget it any way, what's the difference." Economics, he says, "supply and demand, that's it." What about business, simple, "you buy something and sell it for more."[1]

If you think about it, much of our own personal development is similar to a five-minute university. When you attend a workshop, for example, there is a good chance that you are going to retain very little beyond maybe one or two things. When you read a book, you may know how it made you feel, but little is usually learned. We always have good intentions and for the first few days after the workshop or reading a book, we remember some of what we were taught, but as soon as we get back to the office and back to the day-to-day business, anything we gained rapidly starts to deteriorate.

The only way to remember more than *¿cómo está usted* and *muy bien* is to apply what you learn. Learning doesn't magically happen because you attended a workshop or read a book; it happens because you create an experience from what you have been taught. You immerse yourself and create experiences that help you learn, remember, and become better.

I have six boys. Four of the six to this point have served missions for my church as young men. They were all sent to foreign countries and, depending on where they served, learned and became fluent in Spanish, French, Italian, and Tahitian. They didn't become fluent in each of their languages by sitting in a classroom; they became fluent because of the experiences they had in the countries where they served. Everyone around them spoke a language different than English, and they had to apply what they learned to get things they needed.

Leadership development is no different. If we fail to commit to applying what we learn through the experiences we have and fail to change our behavior as a result, then little is learned. Nothing you learn about leadership is really learned, unless you are changing your behavior. A change in behavior as a Care to Lead Leader means you have started to actively and more genuinely begin to serve. It means you are consciously opening (up) more and creating climates of safety and openness. It includes proactively and courageously nurturing those you lead. And it requires you to carefully identify ways to inspire and then to actually inspire. Do you see a theme here? It's about your personal commitment to transferring what you learn to your role as a leader. That seems obvious in some ways, right? But many people have wasted many hours on development activities with little to show for it.

You can't be the best, by practicing like the rest. My kids would regularly roll their eyes when I would say that. But it's true. If you want to be a great leader, you have to be willing to do things no other leaders are doing, and your own personal development is a good place to start.

What's the Plan?

Former American businessman and author Arnold H. Glasgow once said, "An idea not coupled with action will never get any bigger than the brain cell it occupied."[2] The same could be said for what you have learned by reading this book. If you fail to apply the ideas of becoming a Care to Lead Leader, then you significantly lessen your opportunity of becoming one.

You just need to start with a couple of things that you are going to work on. Include the following questions in your plan of applying what you have learned:

- What specifically are you going to work on? What are one to two things you are going to do and change in your leadership to become a Care to Lead Leader?

- How will you do it? What is it going to look like? What are you going to need to do it? What level of commitment is it going to take?

- When will you start? Once you put a date down, you are committed.

- What impact is it going to have on you and those you lead? Clearly see that impact in your mind. Seeing it inspires you to action.

Keep your action plan somewhere you can regularly see it and refer to it. I highly suggest that you use the free action plan template to help you. You can get all of the free tools offered in this book sent to you, along with the Care to Lead Leader action plan template, by going to www.doyoucaretolead.com/tools. Don't wait; create your action plan now.

Conclusion

One sunny day a pig and a chicken were walking down a long road into town. As they were passing one of the local restaurants, the chicken turned to the pig and said, "I have an idea. How about we open up a restaurant?" The pig agreed that was a great idea!

"What will we serve at our restaurant?" the pig asked. "Ham and eggs of course!" said the chicken.

"Whoa, not so fast, Mr. Chicken," said the pig. "While you're simply making a contribution, I'm making a real commitment!"

Your team(s) and organization(s) need you to make a real commitment to becoming a Care to Lead Leader, not just a contribution. They need to know that you care enough to give them, figuratively speaking, your blood, sweat, and tears in everything that you do. They need you to get them excited about the future and stop taking them to predictable, boring, and uninspiring places. Simply maintaining what you have done, are doing, and always will be doing feels more like a contribution, not a real commitment—it's not enough. Your team is depending on you becoming the ham in "eggs and ham."

About 1100 AD, an unknown monk wrote the following:

When I was a young man, I wanted to change the world. I found it was difficult to change the world, so I tried to change my nation. When I found I couldn't change the nation, I began to focus on my town. I couldn't change the town and as an older man, I tried to change my family.

Now, as an old man, I realize the only thing I can change is myself, and suddenly I realize that if long ago I had changed myself, I could have made an impact on my family. My family and I could have made an impact on our town. Their impact could have changed the nation and I could indeed have changed the world.

Do You Care to Lead?

Real commitment starts with *you*. It always starts with you and ripples from there. As a Care to Lead Leader you have a unique and even sacred calling to influence and change lives.

Are you ready? Can you commit to doing these things to become a Care to Lead Leader?

- Thoughtfully and actively **serving** those you lead, as well as others within in your organization

- **Opening up** and creating climates of safety so those that you lead can be more open as well

- Proactively, caringly, and even courageously **nurturing** those you lead

- **Inspiring** those you lead to do more than they ever dreamed of doing

- **Committing** to your team and organization to do everything you can to become the kind of leader others would loyally follow any time to any place

As you work on changing and committing, others on your team will also change and increase their commitment. It truly is a ripple effect: rippling out, but quickly rippling back in and throughout your team and the organization. As you become a Care to Lead Leader, people won't want to take the subway anymore; they are going to quickly acquire a taste for rockets. You now have the formula to take your rockets and those who follow you to places they have never been before.

I wrote this book with the intention of not just writing another leadership book. *Do You Care to Lead?* is a way of life. Are you prepared to make it your way of life?

Care to Lead Leader Commit Takeaways

- Commitment is the binding agent that holds the rest of the Care to Lead Leader formula together.

- Your commitment as a Care to Lead Leader is about not turning back to old habits or old ways; you are now forging new habits and new ways.

- Growth is not optional; personal development is a committed requirement of Care to Lead Leaders.

- Don't let your reading of *Do You Care to Lead?* become a five-minute university.

- If you fail to apply the ideas of becoming a Care to Lead Leader, then you significantly lessen your opportunity of becoming one.

Notes

1. YouTube, "Father Guido Sarducci's Five-Minute University," Video File, January 23, 2007, https://www.youtube.com/watch?v=kO8x8eoU3L4.
2. Arnold H. Glasow, *Brainy Quote,* https://www.brainyquote.com/quotes/arnold_h_glasow_104944.

Acknowledgments

This book would not have been possible without several people. First, I want to thank my wife, Terri. Without her love and support, this book would have never gotten written.

Second, I want to acknowledge and thank David Fares. David is a key reason why I took an interest in leadership many years ago. He is not only a model of servant leadership but also a great friend and mentor as well.

Third, I want to acknowledge a couple of friends, fellow authors, and speakers. Bob Graham not only sent regular research and stories to me but also gets ultimate credit for the title and some of the focus of the book. Thank you, Bob! Mark Macy has been a regular contributor to my blog over the years and several of the stories in *Do You Care to Lead?* are his. Thank you, Mark!

I also want to thank several others who took the time to submit stories, gave me permission to use stories, and/or sent me helpful resources. Thank you, Scott Monge, Stuart Jones, Jeff Fawcett, John Baptista Jr., and Barry Jackson.

Also, thank you to my children and their spouses who asked me on a regular basis how the book was coming along and encouraged me with their kind words.

Finally, I want to acknowledge the newest member of our family—Blue, our Goldendoodle. Though only a puppy, he hung out with me almost every minute in writing this book, providing me with lots of laughs, lots of unconditional love, and lots of stress-relieving breaks. Writing this book would not have been the same without him 😊.

About the Author

Michael G. Rogers is an author and a sought-after Inc. Top 100 Leadership speaker. His first book *You Are the Team: 6 Simple Ways Teammates Can Go from Good to Great* has been used by thousands of companies all over the world in helping build more effective teams. He is a former learning, performance, and quality director for Aetna, a Fortune 50 Company and an adjunct professor in the School of Business at Southern Utah University. Michael resides in Cedar City, Utah, with his wife of 32 years. They are the proud parents of eight children and at this time seven grandchildren, with number eight on the way!

Index

Page references followed by *fig* indicate an illustrated figure.

Deceiving stars team
    members, 90–91, 98–99
Delegating, 114–117
Dickens, Charles, 23
Do as you say, 173–174
Dottie (cleaning lady), 1–2
Duhigg, Charles, 53, 56

E

Edmondson, Amy, 54
"Eggs and ham" story,
    193–194
Eisenhower, Dwight D.,
    2–3, 105
Elizabeth II, Queen, 45
Emotional contagion
    description of, 152
    impact of friends on,
        152–153
    Place of 1,000 Mirrors
        story on, 151–152
    studies on teams
        and, 153
    Twitter study on, 152
Emotions
    emotional contagion, 152
    emotional value of a tweet
        study on, 152
    fear, 100–102
Empathy, 120–121
Employees. *See* Your people
Empowering others
    clarify what empowerment
        does and does not
        mean, 117
    generating the trust
        required for, 115–116

help them feel safe as part
    of, 117
nurturing means,
    114–117
provide proper training
    and tools for, 116–117
provide support,
    encouragement, and
    praise for, 117
Encouraging others, 117
Endorphins, 25
Eye Contact, 113

F

Failure
    Jim Joyce admitting his
        mistake, 60
    Job applicants study
        on admitting
        mistakes, 61
    learning to walk learning
        and, 63
    Sara Blakely's story on
        "reframing," 62
Falling star team members,
    90, 92
Father Guido Sarducci
    ("Saturday Night Live"
    character), 190–191
Fears
    care more about those you
        lead than what you,
        100–102
    Kelli's fear for her brother
        Jeff, 101
Feedback, 67–69
Ferrara, Emilio, 152

The why (or purpose)
  motivation driven by, 139
  questions to discuss to
    define team's, 140
  your team needs to have,
    138–139
WIIFM ("what's in it for
  me?"), 139
"Winton's children" story, 45
Winton, Sir Nicholas, 45–46
Work ethic, 171

Y
Yang, Zeyao, 152
*You Are the Team: 6 Simple
  Ways Teammates Can
  Go from Good to Great*
  (Rogers), 47, 150–151

Your people
  care more about them than
    what your fear, 100–102
  expressing gratitude to,
    168–171
  how you make them
    feel, 173
  provide help, delegate,
    and empower, 114–117
  recognizing and
    rewarding, 117, 157,
    161–167, 170–171
  spending time with,
    105–109
  taking them on rocket
    rides, 5–6
  See also Care to Lead
    Leaders; Nurturing

BRING MICHAEL TO SPEAK AT YOUR NEXT EVENT

Michael is an Inc. Top 100 Leadership Speaker

With over 20 years of experience in building leaders and teams, Michael is a great choice for keynotes and workshops.

"As a result of Mike's training I have developed dramatically as a leader. But more importantly my team is more effective and more unified as a result of the training." ~Eric Leavitt, CEO of the 10th largest privately held insurance brokerage in the US

MichaelGRogers.com